eBook: 9798230799290

Paperback ISBN: 9798230517665

Hardback ISBN: 9798304226592

The Redemptive Story of Christmas

It trumps all others. It is still redemptive and still relevant. God is still working out His purpose in humanity.

Every good gift and every perfect gift is from above and cometh down from the Father of lights, with whom there is no variableness, neither shadow of turning (James 1:17).

G. M. DAVIDSON

Table of Contents

Dedication

I dedicate this book as the first fruit to my Lord and Savior Jesus Christ, to all those who are still waiting for His glorious appearing and to Janice, a woman who knew about waiting patiently.

A note of thanks

Special thanks to Cathy who encouraged me throughout this virgin voyage, to Jolene who motivated me to self-publish, and to Faye without whose help I would not have been able to put my heart on the pages of this book.

Scriptures

All Scriptures quoted in this book are taken from either the King James, the English Standard, or the New King James versions of the Bible.

Preface

MY PURPOSE IN WRITING this book was not clear at first, but as I began to read Luke's narrative my curiosity about the characters was aroused. My focus changed from a group invitation to a more personal study.

The overarching question for me was: What kept these people hopeful year after year until their expectation was fulfilled in the birth of Jesus Christ? It was purposeful consistency in acting on what they believed to be true—teachings handed down to them and temple worship.

Introduction

There is no easy way to withdraw from the crowd at Christmas. It is the busiest and most person-centered season of the year. Not showing up for a family gathering or a Christmas party is unacceptable. It is far more ethical to show up late and leave early or you will hear about it for the next ten years at family gatherings.

Such was December 2023 for me. I was volunteering with Operation Christmas Child in Atlanta, Georgia, packing shoeboxes to send to the country of Chad, when I received a text message from a friend in south Florida. The banner on my cell phone highlighted the gist of the message, which read, "Grace, I am inviting you to join us in reading the Christmas story in the Gospel of Luke with our Life group this Christmas."

"I would love to," I wrote back quickly, intent on thinking about it when I got off work later that evening.

Luke!

What up-and-coming author like me, would refuse to sit at the feet of the man who wrote most of the New Testament? Moreover, I had maintained a serious crush on Dr. Luke since I first met him in high school while studying the Acts of the Apostles. Lisa Harper, one of my favorite Bible storytellers, would always intertwine her crushes on dead theologians in her telling. *Well, Lisa, my friend, you are not alone*, I said in my head, looking around to see if anyone at the table had been troubled by the seemingly inappropriate smile on my face. I know Luke tells his stories unlike any of his counterparts. I hope to show you what I mean by that later.

But once I hit "Send" there would be no retreat. Where would I find time to do this? I was already committed to a daily 5:00 a.m. prayer call that lasted roughly an hour. Then I would spend another hour or two in my personal devotion time, which is a must-do. This simple act of spending alone-time with God was not easy to establish. I had to be intentional and persevering and had to learn not to beat myself up about it when I did not get up in time to do my personal study a morning or two. After fourteen years, thankfully it had become a cherished routine in my day. If you and I don't command our mornings and set the tone for our day, I promise you that someone else will. The choice is yours.

That night, as I curled up on the sofa in the hotel room with a cup of hot tea, I began to think about people who isolated themselves to spend time alone with God. There were only a few, as far as I knew. The Apostle Paul immediately came to mind. He was born in the Turkish province of Mersin in the city of Tarsus to Jewish parents who named him Saul. His parents were descendants of the tribe of Benjamin and may have named him after King Saul who was also a Benjamite, (1 Samuel 9:1; Philippians 3:5). Who would think that Saul would grow up and become associated with persecuting Christians?

In my study of the book of the Acts of the Apostles, Paul comes across as a Roman soldier on a rampage to kill Christians. In my own quest to bridge the gaps in what we know about him, I use my imagination.

I imagine Saul of Tarsus as a brilliant, young Pharisee who graduated from the University of Tarsus at the very top of his class. I see him dressed in a black suit, tailcoat flying, and one hand holding his hat onto his head as he runs off campus all the way to the synagogue. He's thinking about what he will say to the men he will meet with afterward. He wants to be just like his dad (Acts 23.6). He begins something like:

> *These radicals are growing in numbers; they speak of a King! We have no King. Saul is long dead. I am a Jew by heritage, but I am a Roman citizen by birth. This group has the audacity to call themselves "The Way." They do not know the way or the truth. Judaism is truth. Who do these people think they are? I will show them!*

Saul would imprison, threaten, interrogate, and kill first-century Christ-followers (Acts 8:3, Acts 9:1). He was also the man who would consent to the stoning death of young Stephen, a Greek-Jewish convert called a Hellenist because he still held some Greek traditions. Stephen defended his position in Christ with such brilliance that the Sanhedrin Jews were often infuriated. In his speech, he reminded them of Moses's saying, "The Lord thy God will raise up unto thee a Prophet unto thee from the midst of thee. Of thy brethren, like unto me; unto him ye shall hearken" (Deuteronomy 18:15). Stephen became the church's first martyr.

After the stoning death of Stephen, the group known as The Way grew even more but so did Saul's hatred for the new converts. He perceived them as a threat to Judaism while the Roman Empire was threatened by their influence. Saul believed killing their leader, Jesus, should have sent this little band of Wayfarers into hiding for good. But they kept popping right back up again, infusing others with their doctrine. Saul's hatred for this group pulsed through his body like venom. He would hunt and find them wherever they were hiding. This led him on a journey to Damascus.

With his men, Saul left Jerusalem on a trail of blinding dust on a sunshiny day, cracking a whip onto the hide of his steed. Suddenly, like a scene straight out of a John Wayne movie. a beam of light frightened the horse and threw its rider, Saul. The horse reared up on its hind legs with majestic power, hovering over Saul's body long enough for him to roll beneath its belly before its hooves slammed into the ground.

"Saul, Saul, why persecutes thou me?" God asked.

Saul could not answer. After all, he had no idea it was God he was chasing. He was looking for the people who followed the teachings of Jesus. Saul, the bounty hunter, blinded by a strange light and thrown from his horse, was led into the city of Damascus. That night, he had a strange dream in which he learned he would be left to the mercy of the very people he was persecuting.

"...And when I could not see for the glory of that light, being led by the hand of them that were with me, I came into Damascus" (Acts 22:11).

This single, overpowering act of God led to Saul's conversion from sinner to saved. Paul would change his name from Saul to Paul. Biblical apologists claim Paul changed his name to reflect his transformation and to be "all things to all people" (1 Corinthians 9:19–23). I credit God for Saul's name change as a result of that dramatic encounter on the road to Damascus.

This example highlights the benefits of praying before studying. Ask the Lord to illuminate your mind through the work of the Holy Spirit. This is vital because Bible scholars have different schools of thought on the same passages of Scripture. Name changes are just one example. You will read of name changes throughout the Bible. Pay attention to the context within which they occur: Who? What? Where? When? and Why? You will observe that some were done by men and others by God. The name changes done by men like Pharaoh Neco, who changed Eliakim's name to Joiakim, was merely to show his control over him. This is why praying before studying is beneficial.

When God is behind a name change, there is always lasting evidence of a life-changing encounter with Him. The individual assumes a new identity and a separation from the cacophony of life. In Saul's case, he emerged after his separation and was introduced as Paul for the first time in Acts 13:9: "Saul who is also called Paul ..." From there on, he was referred to as Paul (Acts 13:13). He had retreated from persecuting God's people and had become a Christ-follower himself.

Stephen's Gate. Retrieved from The Bible Journey (public domain).

AFTER SAUL PUBLICLY confessed his faith and accepted Jesus Christ as Lord and Savior, God commissioned him to be a light to the Gentile people, the underdogs of society according to ancient teachings. Saul was ready but he was not equipped. "Not so fast," said Barnabas, the man who would vouch for Paul's newfound faith in Christ and would later introduce him to their leader, Peter, and the group of Wayfarers. Paul had emerged from his three years of solitary study of the life and ministry of Christ. The man who had given the order to kill Stephen, and who had held the coats of the men who stoned him to death, was himself completely dead. "Neither went I up to Jerusalem to them which were apostles before me, but I went into Arabia and returned again unto Damascus. Then after three years I went up to Jerusalem to see Peter and stayed with him fifteen days" (Galatians 1:17–18).

The point of this story is worth its weight in gold. People will make time for what is important to them. Here, Paul is reinforcing the importance of solitude, of time alone with God. During those three soul-searching years, when he reviewed the ancient Hebrew writings of the prophets, God revealed Jesus Christ to him. Paul became an Apostle of Jesus Christ and penned these words on the tablet of his heart: "That I may know him, and the power of his resurrection, and the fellowship of his sufferings, being made conformable unto his death: if by any means I might attain unto the resurrection of the dead" (Philippians 3:10).

I had no idea what reading this story would do for me, After all, I had read it so many times that one more time would certainly not hurt me. Surely my friend was not asking me to do anything crazy, like the Stylites who, during the Byzantine period, lived on a pillar of stone for decades. Time alone within public view is attention-seeking behavior and would not have provided me the private moments with God I needed.

Neither was my friend asking me to give up wealth, which I did not have, unlike Saint Francis of Assisi (1181–1226). In the History and Society section of Britannica's website, Lawrence Cunningham describes the life and legacy of the Catholic friar. Saint Francis was born while his father was away from home, so his mother christened him Giovanni di Bernardone in honor of John the Baptist. His dad called him Francesco, later changing his name officially to Pietro di Bernardone.

Francesco grew up an unrestrained Italian youth who was captured as a prisoner of war in the battle between Assisi and Perugia. In prison, Francesco patiently waited for his father to pay his ransom. In a cold, dark cell at night, Francis started having visions of his heavenly Father, God. He heard God telling him to do something specific: "Build my church."

He left prison, thinking God meant a physical building. His attempt to steal money from his father, a wealthy merchant, led to his isolation from society. Francesco, as his father called him, abandoned his former life of luxury and indulgence for one of poverty, caring for animals and the leprous outcasts of society. His search for intimacy with the Lord God would lead to his conversion to Christianity. Giovanni di Pietro di Bernardone was canonized as Saint Francis of Assisi on July 16, 1228.

As I recounted these epic stories, I asked myself, What was the common thread between these men? They were both converted to the cause of Christ. They both had a supernatural encounter, and they met men and women who fed them and supported them along the way and their lives were never the same again. I drifted off to sleep in wonderment! What about women? Were there many who waited in hope or who encountered the Son of the living God as these men did? Who would bridge the gap between the ancient hope and the New Testament hope of experiencing God? An iconostasis act of the continuation was recorded by the old prophets in Isaiah 40:3–5 and Malachi 3:1, 4–5.

The clock blared repeatedly until I woke up. I was still on the sofa. My back felt like it could use a chiropractor right away. I reached for my Bible, already opened to Luke, where I read the introduction and found my answer. It was the timing. Luke did something that had never been done before: He gave an account of the life of Christ in his own unique way. He gave an incredible account from a historical perspective that no one could dispute. Mathew did the same thing for the Jewish naysayers in the book that bears his name. Similarly, Luke did this for his Gentile folks, in a way that would be beneficial to all new converts. Theophilus, the person Luke addressed, needed more convincing evidence that Christ was who he claimed to be!

This would be my takeaway from Luke's account of Christmas: *It is the retelling of the miraculous birth of a baby boy who is still sharing the gift of His redemptive work on the cross of Calvary year after year. His story will never grow old, and His gift can never be aborted.*

"For all have sinned and come short of the glory of God" (Romans 3:23). The miracle of salvation will remain alive and well forever.

Introducing Luke

Three of the twelve Jewish men who followed Jesus throughout his ministry wrote about him: Matthew, Mark, and James, Jesus' brother who wrote both the books of James and Jude.

Yet, a Gentile who knew nothing about this Jesus of Nazareth, who was converted in the early church, would write most of the New Testament. This non-Jewish writer would pen the book bearing his name. He did not stop there but continued to follow the post-resurrection happenings from the phenomenal outpouring of the Holy Spirit fifty days after the Passover recorded in the book of Acts. He was a faithful companion to the Apostle Paul on his three missionary journeys and in shipwrecks, and he was a trusted attending physician to the Apostle while he was under house arrest. This writer's name is Luke.

In the Acts of the Apostles, Luke demonstrates an extraordinary understanding of the work of the Holy Spirit that is unparalleled by any other New Testament writer. His research documents a unique perspective on the birth, ministry, trial, crucifixion, death, burial, and resurrection of Jesus Christ.

Authorship

G od is the author. The early writings of men like Justin Martyr and Tertullian authenticated Luke's writings and even his background, stating that he was "not of the circumcision." Circumcision is a Jewish custom in which the foreskin of the male infant is removed eight days after birth.

Gentiles were notorious enemies of the Jews; thus, it is significant that they did not adhere to Jewish practices. Luke was a well-educated man and a physician, as verified in Colossians 4:14. He traveled extensively with the Apostle Paul to whom he owed his conversion to Christianity. Paul was a brilliant scholar steeped in Judaism and was influenced by the teachings of Rabbi Gamaliel. I had a beautiful reminder at a revival meeting at our church a year ago that God is the author of the Scriptures; this makes Luke, as a New Testament writer, simply an instrument of God (2 Timothy 3:16–17; Psalms 119:89).

Approximate dates of compilation

THE APPROXIMATE DATE of Luke's writing remains a debate among Bible scholars. Some center their dates around Jesus's prediction of the fall of Jerusalem (Luke 21:20). It is well established that the siege of Jerusalem took place in AD 70. The Romans destroyed the city and tore the temple apart brick by brick, searching for gold.

Historically, pirates had been notorious for hiding their plunder in churches. Several years ago, on a tour of Panama City, Panama, I was blown away by the beautiful golden pillars bracing the walls of a cathedral. These pillars remain a lasting display of the gold pirates had lavished on the church in the Caribbean. This paled in comparison to the display of gold in King Herod's temple.

At the time of Luke's writing, the temple Herod demolished had not been rebuilt. Scholars feel safe in estimating Luke's writings were compiled between AD 80 and AD 110. To this day, the temple has not been rebuilt, and all that is left of its former glory is the Western Wall known as the "Wailing Wall." This is the same wall where orthodox Jews still gather to pray daily. Presently, a mosque sits on the site.

It is also the site, according to the book of Revelation, on which Jesus will set his feet when he returns to earth. This site is known as the Temple Mount. The book of Revelation (Greek: *apocalypses;* English: apocalypse), is the revelation of Jesus Christ to a human recipient—in this case John, his last surviving disciple, as all the others had been killed. Jesus is showing him the catastrophic end of the world as we know it and the beginning of a new one.

How to get the most out of this study

PRAY FIRST, AND INVITE Jesus into your life, your heart, your mind, and your study. The book of Proverbs reminds us of this simple truth: "Trust in the Lord with all thine heart and lean not on your own understanding. In all thy ways acknowledge him, and he shall direct thy path" (Proverbs 3:5–6).

Many years ago, I sold Amway products to make extra money as I was a single parent. I enjoyed doing the presentations in my apartment because I could involve my kids instead of dropping them off at the babysitter. At one Amway conference, I met Jim Rohn. He used so many quotes to nail his point, I would say, that's a write-down. Here is one that is relevant and still worth doing our best to live up to: Don't wish for less challenge, wish for more wisdom. James, the brother of Jesus reminds us in James 1:5 not to be afraid to ask for it. God assures the ones who ask that he will give it generously.

Invite the Holy Spirit, as the third part of the Godhead, into your study and ask Him to direct and lead your time with Him. Ask the Holy Spirit to reveal truths in His Word to your heart and mind so you will become more like Him (Philippians 2:5–11).

Here are some practical things to remember when preparing for a Bible study.

1. You will need pen and paper. Many of you attend

conferences for work or personal growth and you hear powerful speakers like Tony Robbins, one of the most energetic speakers on the planet. He tells his attendees to take notes like you are going to teach it to someone else. Take lots of notes as you read, and search for more information as if you are going to share them with your children or a Sunday school class. You never know so just write down things that leap out at you in your studies.

2. You will need a good Bible with cross references. I use *Nelson's Complete Study Bible*. I highly recommend the most ancient writings as the foundation. The King James version is the most preserved of the species. It is written in prose and highly poetic language. I love it. If you are English- speaking and desire a more modern translation, I highly recommend the English Standard Version (ESV). If you speak another language, then use the closest translation to the original preserved copy of the Bible. The debate is that, as more scrolls are found, the more the Bible is updated and made more relevant and easier to read. It is wonderful that more scrolls are being excavated but the question is, How holy and inspired are the words of these emerging scribes? The next time you go into the bank and the teller holds up a one-hundred-dollar bill, ask the teller how they identify counterfeit bills. Apply that principle in life.

3. You will also need additional tools to cross reference like Strong's *The Exhaustive Concordance of the Bible*

and a Bible dictionary such as *The Expanded Vine's Expository Dictionary of New Testament Words*.

4. Another useful tool is *The Holman Illustrated Bible*, which is based on the Byzantine majority text with footnotes and is similar to the New King James Version.

5. If you are a visual learner, an illustrated Bible with maps will bring these locations to life. If you are savvy with technology, use the internet to find the geographical location of the areas you are learning about. Look at the terrain and note if it is flat or hilly. Find out what crops are suitable for that climate and the mode of transportation used. All of this helps to put the passages of Scripture we read into proper context. I hope you will find the beauty of the terrain embedded within the context of Luke's narrative as you travel, live, and worship. Then try to apply this to any piece of literary work you read hereafter.

6. You will need a plan for handling difficult questions and passages of Scripture. If you decide to become a student of the Word of God, you will definitely have questions. Ask God first. Then ask your pastor. I mean that sincerely. Get in the mindset of asking God first. It is a practice that you can begin at any age and any stage of your life. I started the practice late in life with the help of my friend, Lorna, who always stopped me in the middle of our conversations and say, "Grace, did you ask the Lord?" and "What did he say?" At first, I was so taken aback at that reality that my response would be truthful: "You know we

humans have an innate tendency to help God." We are so impatient. That is why I was so impressed by the patience of Anna, the prophetess.

We all need an inner circle of friends who will keep us accountable and who will ask hard questions—like, Did you ask the Lord first? and Did you wait for His response before you made your first move?—until talking to God first about everything becomes a practice. Along with this habit of asking God comes the most important thing: knowing His voice. It is through the alone times spent in His presence that we learn to listen and to attend to our own affairs rather than keeping every waking moment preoccupied with social media and other platforms. Thank you, Lorna.

The practice of waiting for a response is an entirely different ball game.

When the Angel told Mary that she was with child, Mary asked, "How could this be seeing that I know not a man?" The Angel Gabriel replied, "The Holy Spirit will come upon you, and the power of the Highest will overshadow you, therefore also, that holy thing which shall be born of thee shall be shall be called the son of God. " Luke 1:34–35. Sometimes the response you get to your question may not satisfy the deep longing in your spirit to understand it all. Mary kept the things about her pregnancy she did not understand in her heart and mused about them.

In my Bible readings, I often encounter things I don't entirely understand, such as the story recorded in John 8:1–11. A woman was caught in adultery, an act that involved two people, not one. The Pharisees and leaders dragged only the woman to Jesus. They insisted that she should be stoned to death as it was the law. She is presented as the one who solicited the act, so her reputation was at stake. This woman was brought to Jesus to make a mockery of his ministry and to shame the woman. This story begs the question, Where is the man?

According to the law, both the man and the woman should have been stoned to death (Leviticus 20:10; Deuteronomy 22:22). Where was her partner in crime? If you ask your pastor, or small group leader, it is guaranteed that they have a theological answer based on their view of canonicity. This story uses the word "caught" in the very act of a *Pericope Adulterae,* an example of a *hapax legomenon*—which is just a descriptor for a word or phrase that is mentioned only once in the Bible. Some theologians still argue that John did not include this story in his original writings and that the language is more like Luke's writing ... seriously? Is that the problem, really?

While leaders debated under whose name (John's or Luke's) this story should be canonized, there was no doubt that inspired men knew God demanded it must be included in holy writings. Here is why: This remains a universal moral issue. God foreknew the problem would not be just a first-century dilemma. The abortion issue of our day raises the same question: Where are the men who brought you here? Silence.

Jesus looked around at the men who circled the woman and who held rocks ready to throw at her. They had dragged her through the streets; the hem of her skirt was lined with its dirt and filth. They threw her at Jesus's feet, then encircled her and Jesus. There was no escape. She was guilty and she was alone. Jesus was forced to confront the issue.

I often wonder when men will begin to take responsibility for their role in the woman's dilemma. Like the Levitical law, our laws still hold the woman responsible for an act that involves two people: a man and a woman. Go figure. Only Jesus can adequately answer that ancient question. No theological, political, or philosophical ideologies can adequately respond to moral dilemmas like this one. Much to the chagrin of the crowd, Jesus, the moral lawgiver, responded with compassion: "Go thy way and sin no more" (John 8:11). Like Mary, the mother of Jesus, we can only ponder some things in our hearts.

Talk through the tough points!

I STRONGLY ENCOURAGE guided discourse in the home. Home is about the only place where free speech can occur without political correctness. Our institutions of higher learning are shying away from critical collegiate discourse, a First Amendment right in the United States of America. The home, therefore, provides a safe place for children and young adults to discuss and analyze any topic critically. There are ways to listen, to respond, and to steer the discussion to broader ideas without biting remarks or using colorful expletives.

Discourse requires practice. If all else fails, call a time-out and stop the conversation. Excuse yourself. Then change your activity, change physiology, go for a long walk, clear your thoughts, and try to understand from the other person's perspective. Taking deep breaths will cause a gradual release of endorphins that will ultimately replace the adrenaline rush and build-up of disease-forming cortisol levels in your bloodstream.

Upon returning, don't rehash the triggers; sincerely apologize where applicable, and let the proverbial dust settle. Laugh at yourselves. If you have the tenacity of a bulldog that latches on to everything, learn to let things go and move on. I suggest expressing your thoughts on paper. Write a letter to the person who least understood your views or journal the entire conversation as you recall it. Always seek to understand the other person more than you strive to be understood, a principle I learned during a Stephen Covey workshop years ago. Continue your personal study of the Scriptures. Rest assured that as you draw near God, he will draw near to you; that is a promise James documented in James 4:8.

Texts used in this study

THE BIBLE VERSIONS used for this study are the King James "Authorized" version of 1611, the New King James Version (1982), and the English Standard Version (2001).

Most copies of the Bible written for English-speaking people are preserved from ancient Hebrew Masoretic readings of the first Rabbinic Bible, edited by Felix Pratensis in 1517–1518. In addition, preserved texts are from the second Rabbinic Bible, edited by Jacob Ben Chayyim and printed by Daniel Bomberg in 1525. The New Testament is solely based on the Greek text.

John Wycliffe (c.1330–1384), and William Tyndale (c.1490/94–1536) translated the Bible from Hebrew and Greek manuscripts into modern English vernacular. For this work, they were declared heretics. Wycliff died of a stroke. His bones were exhumed and burned sometime later. Tyndale was arrested in 1536, strangled, then burnt at the stake.

The kings of England, starting with Henry VIII, were determined to break away from the Catholic Church and so ushered in Protestantism. Since Catholic priests used the Latin Vulgate to lead Mass and the common man could not read this text, the need for a common English text arose.

At long last, James I of England followed through; he spared no expense to complete the translation of the Hebrew text into the English language for his English-speaking people. Thus, the "King James" title of the English Bible is attributed to his memory. The most important takeaway from this story is that the Bible is now available to the public. The common farmer can read the Bible as well as any elite priest. It is still the Father's pleasure to give us what we do not deserve.

Prior to this, priests used the Latin Vulgate text to lead Mass. Desiderius Erasmus, the Dutch theologian, initiated the reformative work within the Holy Roman Empire round 1500. Martin Luther, a professor of moral theology, continued the works Erasmus started when he nailed his Ninety-Five Theses, *A Disputation on the Power and Efficacy of Indulgences* on the door of the Wittenberg Cathedral in 1517.

Many argue that the classical approach to a literary translation of the Hebrew Textus Receptus makes reading the King James Bible challenging. For me personally, it is a matter of preference. I wouldn't have it any other way as I grew up reciting Shakespeare's *As You Like It* and patting my Afro hairdo in place while getting dressed for school in the mornings.

Readers ask hard questions that must be answered intelligently to the best of the Believer's knowledge. These are questions like, What about errors? I respond that there are variants in every text; however, the Word of God is inerrant and is not rife with as many variants as the Greek translations. Itis inspired and "profitable for doctrine, reproof, correction, and instruction in righteousness . . ." (2 Timothy 3:16).

The readings for this study, Luke, Chapters 1–3, will precede the backstories. Too much evidence is at our fingertips to support the Bible and the God of the Bible or to refute it. Only never let it be said of you, as it was of the atheist philosopher Bertrand Russell, who was asked, "If you meet God after you die, what will you say to Him to justify your unbelief?" Russell responded, "I will tell Him He did not give me enough evidence."

Here are just a few resources for you.

Boogert, E. (2015). The Origin of the Byzantine Text: New perspectives in a deadlocked debate. *Pthu.* https://www.academia.edu/10303182/The_Origin_of_the_Byzantine_Text_New_Perspectives_in_a_D

Breshears. Jefrey D. *Introduction to Bibliology: What Every Christian Should Know about the Origins, Composition, Inspiration, Interpretation, Canonicity, and Transmission of the Bible.* Wipf and Stock, 2017.

White, James R. *The King James Only Controversy: Can You Trust Modern Translations?* Bethany House, 2009.

Enough said. Let's dig in.

The First Chapter of Luke's Gospel

1 Forasmuch as many have taken in hand to set forth in order a declaration of those things which are most surely believed among us,

2 Even as they delivered them unto us, which from the beginning were eyewitnesses, and ministers of the word.

3 It seemed good to me also, having had perfect understanding of all things from the very first, to write unto thee in order, most excellent Theophilus,

4 That thou mightest know the certainty of those things, wherein thou hast been instructed.

5 There was in the days of Herod, the king of Judaea, a certain priest named Zacharias, of the course of Abia: and his wife was of the daughters of Aaron, and her name was Elisabeth.

6 And they were both righteous before God, walking in all the commandments and ordinances of the Lord blameless.

7 And they had no child, because that Elisabeth was barren, and they both were now well stricken in years.

8 And it came to pass, that while he executed the priest's office before God in the order of his course,

9 According to the custom of the priest's office, his lot was to burn incense when he went into the temple of the Lord.

10 And the whole multitude of the people were praying without at the time of incense.

11 And there appeared unto him an angel of the Lord standing on the right side of the altar of incense.

12 And when Zacharias saw him, he was troubled, and fear fell upon him.

13 But the angel said unto him, Fear not, Zacharias: for thy prayer is heard; and thy wife Elisabeth shall bear thee a son, and thou shalt call his name John.

14 And thou shalt have joy and gladness; many shall rejoice at his birth.

15 For he shall be great in the sight of the Lord and shall drink neither wine nor strong drink; and he shall be filled with the Holy Ghost, even from his mother's womb.

16 And many of the children of Israel shall he turn to the Lord their God.

17 And he shall go before him in the spirit and power of Elias, to turn the hearts of the fathers to the children, and the disobedient to the wisdom of the just; to make ready a people prepared for the Lord.

18 And Zacharias said unto the angel, Whereby shall I know this? for I am an old man, and my wife well stricken in years.

19 And the angel answering said unto him, I am Gabriel, that stand in the presence of God; and am sent to speak unto thee, and to shew thee these glad tidings.

20 And, behold, thou shalt be dumb, and not able to speak, until the day that these things shall be performed, because thou believest not my words, which shall be fulfilled in their season.

21 And the people waited for Zacharias, and marveled that he tarried so long in the temple.

22 And when he came out, he could not speak unto them: and they perceived that he had seen a vision in the temple: for he beckoned unto them and remained speechless.

23 And it came to pass, that, as soon as the days of his ministration were accomplished, he departed to his own house.

24 And after those days his wife Elisabeth conceived, and hid herself five months, saying,

25 Thus hath the Lord dealt with me in the days wherein he looked on me, to take away my reproach among men.

26 And in the sixth month the angel Gabriel was sent from God unto a city of Galilee, named Nazareth,

27 To a virgin espoused to a man whose name was Joseph, of the house of David; and the virgin's name was Mary.

28 And the angel came in unto her, and said, Hail, thou that art highly favored, the Lord is with thee: blessed art thou among women.

29 And when she saw him, she was troubled at his saying, and cast in her mind what manner of salutation this should be.

30 And the angel said unto her, Fear not, Mary: for thou hast found favour with God.

31 And, behold, thou shalt conceive in thy womb, and bring forth a son, and shalt call his name JESUS.

32 He shall be great, and shall be called the Son of the Highest: and the Lord God shall give unto him the throne of his father David:

33 And he shall reign over the house of Jacob forever; and of his kingdom there shall be no end.

34 Then said Mary unto the angel, How shall this be, seeing I know not a man?

35 And the angel answered and said unto her, The Holy Ghost shall come upon thee, and the power of the Highest shall overshadow thee: therefore also that holy thing which shall be born of thee shall be called the Son of God.

36 And, behold, thy cousin Elisabeth, she hath also conceived a son in her old age: and this is the sixth month with her, who was called barren.

37 For with God nothing shall be impossible.

38 And Mary said, Behold the handmaid of the Lord; be it unto me according to thy word. And the angel departed from her.

39 And Mary arose in those days, and went into the hill country with haste, into a city of Juda.

40 And entered into the house of Zacharias, and saluted Elisabeth.

41 And it came to pass, that, when Elisabeth heard the salutation of Mary, the babe leaped in her womb; and Elisabeth was filled with the Holy Ghost:

42 And she spake out with a loud voice, and said, Blessed art thou among women, and blessed is the fruit of thy womb.

43 And whence is this to me, that the mother of my Lord should come to me?

44 For, lo, as soon as the voice of thy salutation sounded in mine ears, the babe leaped in my womb for joy.

45 And blessed is she that believed: for there shall be a performance of those things which were told her from the Lord.

46 And Mary said, My soul doth magnify the Lord,

47 And my spirit hath rejoiced in God my Saviour.

48 For he hath regarded the low estate of his handmaiden: for, behold, from henceforth all generations shall call me blessed.

49 For he that is mighty hath done to me great things; and holy is his name.

50 And his mercy is on them that fear him from generation to generation.

51 He hath shewed strength with his arm; he hath scattered the proud in the imagination of their hearts.

52 He hath put down the mighty from their seats, and exalted them of low degree.

53 He hath filled the hungry with good things; and the rich he hath sent empty away.

54 He hath helped his servant Israel, in remembrance of his mercy;

55 As he spake to our fathers, to Abraham, and to his seed forever.

56 And Mary abode with her about three months, and returned to her own house.

57 Now Elisabeth's full time came that she should be delivered; and she brought forth a son.

58 And her neighbors and her cousins heard how the Lord had showed great mercy upon her, and they rejoiced with her.

59 And it came to pass, that on the eighth day, they came to circumcise the child; and they called him Zacharias, after the name of his father.

60 And his mother answered and said, Not so; but he shall be called John.

61 And they said unto her, There is none of thy kindred that is called by this name.

62 And they made signs to his father, how he would have him called.

63 And he asked for a writing table, and wrote, saying, His name is John. And they marveled all.

64 And his mouth was opened immediately, and his tongue loosed, and he spake, and praised God.

65 And fear came on all that dwelt round about them: and all these sayings were noised abroad throughout all the hill country of Judaea.

66 And all they that heard them laid them up in their hearts, saying, What manner of child shall this be! And the hand of the Lord was with him.

67 And his father Zacharias was filled with the Holy Ghost, and prophesied, saying,

68 Blessed be the Lord God of Israel; for he hath visited and redeemed his people,

69 And hath raised up an horn of salvation for us in the house of his servant David;

70 As he spake by the mouth of his holy prophets, which have been since the world began:

71 That we should be saved from our enemies, and from the hand of all that hate us.

72 To perform the mercy promised to our fathers, and to remember his holy covenant.

73 The oath which he sware to our father Abraham,

74 That he would grant unto us, that we being delivered out of the hand of our enemies might serve him without fear,

75 In holiness and righteousness before him, all the days of our life.

76 And thou, child, shalt be called the prophet of the Highest: for thou shalt go before the face of the Lord to prepare his ways;

77To give knowledge of salvation unto his people by the remission of their sins,

78 Through the tender mercy of our God; whereby the dayspring from on high hath visited us,

79 To give light to them that sit in darkness and in the shadow of death, to guide our feet into the way of peace.

80 And the child grew, and waxed strong in spirit, and was in the deserts till the day of his shewing unto Israel.

King James Version (KJV, public domain)

Chapter 1

Luke dedicates his work to Theophilus

Here we find Luke presenting his methodical findings on the life, death, and resurrection of our Lord Jesus Christ to a man of high standing who was steeped in the Greek tradition. Why? This man also happened to be a new convert to Christianity who yearned for more evidence to believe the Jesus was indeed who He said He was. Theophilus's need for a solid faith in Christ appears to me a far more intelligent stance than the excuse for unbelief we hear in our postmodern culture, such as: Christians are just a bunch of hypocrites who claim to have higher standards than the rest of us! Well, we ought to! We try hard to! But we often fail, just like you do, my friend. We get back up, dust ourselves off and get back on that steed called Christianity. You are as scared as many of us were. It is just a decision, like everything else in life: marriage, having a baby, going to college—a decision that only you can make, no one else

I often hear it said across the pulpit, and I am going to repeat it here because it is true: "The God-breathed, inspired stories we read in the books of the Bible were not written to us, but for us." The books of the Old Testaments as we know them were written to the Hebrew people. The books of the New Testament were written for the early Christians. Of all the labor-intensive, inspired work of our devout forefathers, only sixty-six books were compiled into what we now called the Holy Bible, *the Greatest Book ever written.*

Dr. Luke, like his mentors, assumed the classical approach in his writings. Here is an irresistible sample of one of his mentors, Epaphroditus, that will whet your literary appetite for details:

> In the former book, most honored Epaphroditus, I have demonstrated our antiquity and confirmed the truth of what I have said from the writings of the Phoenicians, the Chaldeans, and the Egyptians. I have moreover produced many of the Grecian writers as witnesses thereto.

> (Flavius Josephus. *The Antiquities of the* Jews, Book 2. p. 951. Translated by William Whiston. A.M. Thomas Nelson, Inc. 1998).

This is Luke's approach as he began his letter to Theophilus.

> Dear Theophilus,

> 1. Forasmuch as many have taken in hand to set in order a declaration of those things which are most surely believed among us,

> 2. Even as they delivered them unto us, which from the beginning were eyewitnesses, and ministers of the word;

3. It seemed good to me also, having had perfect understanding of all things from the very first, to write unto thee in order, most excellent Theophilus,

4. That you may know the certainty of those things, wherein which thou hast been instructed.

(Luke 1:1–4)

In today's vernacular it might be:

Sir, like me, you are a Gentile, and a new convert to this movement called "The Way." We both need a better understanding of why this Jew, called Jesus, was hated so much by his own people. Most honored Theophilus, here are my authoritative accounts of what Jesus said and did as written by his disciples, eyewitnesses, and leaders of the movement. I am convinced that his own people crucified him for no earthly reason. Unbelievable!

Luke begins his story properly by establishing a timeline: "There was in days of Herod, the King of Judea, a certain priest named Zacharias, of the division of Abijah, his wife was of the daughters of Aaron, and her name was Elisabeth" (Luke 1:5). Herod was a name given to a group of men who became a strong dynasty of rulers. Many of Herod's appointments resulted from his alliance with Roman leaders like Emperor Augustus. Augustus appointed the narcissistic Herod the Great, who named all his offspring Herod.

When Herod the Great died in 4 BC, his son, Herod Antipas, was appointed tetrarch, governor over a quarter of his father's kingdom. Herod of Antipas's rule would then last from 4 BC to 39 AD. This is the Herod to watch as he becomes a thorn in the sides of the ministries of both John the Baptist and Jesus Christ. Luke discovered why this king, who had everything a person could want, was so insecure in such a lofty position. The birth of Jesus would pose such a threat to Rome and to Herod that he would have every child two years of age and under slain. He was trying so hard to kill not the unborn, but children who had been born who were two years old or younger. Still innocent, mind you! Read Luke 3:19–20; 9:7–10; 13:31–33.

The timelines and the happenings make the Bible irrefutable. In the Old Testament, after King David recovered the ark from the Philistines, he decided to build a house for it. Unfortunately, the Lord revealed through the prophet Nathan that David was not the one to build him a temple but it was to be his son, Solomon. David was disappointed but he trusted God enough to help with the preparations.

One thing David did was to expand the division of priesthood with the help of Zadok and Ahimalek. The priests continued the practice of casting lots to ensure fairness. David designated the Aaronite division of priests and Levites to their duties. The eighth lot fell on Abijah, who was assigned to lead the celebrations of the rebuilding of the walls around the temple. (I Chronicles 24:7–10, Tanak [Ketuvim]. p. 1564).

Abijah's selection is relevant to Luke's telling because Zacharias, father of John the Baptist, traditionally belonged to this division of Levite priests. Both Zacharias and his wife Elisabeth belonged to the priestly descendants of Aaron (Luke 1:5).

Throughout the book of Luke, you will see remarkable timelines—based on evidence of Roman leadership, sieges, and occupation, such as the siege of Jerusalem—as infallible proof that Christ was born, lived, died, and was resurrected from the dead. Jesus would fulfill prophecies spoken about his life by Isaiah and others more than 700 years before his arrival on the scene. I respect the gray hairs who went before me—those old folks would say "Stick a pin right there," which meant to pause for a moment. Think about the religious groups today who recruit innocent victims to their false religion under the guise that "Jesus is just another prophet." When anyone would make this claim, whether they knocked at the door or greeted you in the street, my friend Lorna would say, "Ask them this: Of all the prophets who ever lived, which one of them is still alive? See Romans 1:4. How is this dead prophet you worship coming back to raise the quick and the dead?"

The book of Revelation boldly declares, "Behold, I come quickly, and my reward is with me, to give every man according as his work shall be. I am Alpha and Omega, the beginning and the end, the first and the last" (Revelation 22:12–13). Jesus, the great Redeemer of Mankind, lives forever (Job 19:25).

Luke would inadvertently prove to the Jewish community that Jesus is more than a prophet and that the saving grace of Jesus Christ is not based on our performance but is the finished work of the cross. Most importantly, the Sabbath, as the Hebrew people knew it,, would never be the same. The Sabbath would no longer be a day of bloodiness based on the sacrifices of bulls and goats. Some nations, like the Ammonites, went as far as practicing the bloodiness of human sacrifice of their children. What an insult to God, who had made the Sabbath as day for Himself to rest from all His creative work as recorded in the book of Genesis. Mark would remind us that the Sabbath was not meant to burden us, rather it was meant to help us (Mark 3:1–6). We can all benefit from being more intentional about taking a load off to relax and serve each other after a laborious workweek.

To further support his thesis that salvation was not performance-based, Mark recorded incidents where Jesus broke every rule of law the Scribes and Pharisees clung to about the Sabbath. The Sovereign Lord of the Sabbath taught in the synagogues on the Sabbath, healed the sick, and threw our thieves and robbers who were using the church for everything other than a place to worship. The Apostle Paul, in his first letter to the church at Corinth, warned them to stop participating in certain activities. If you are not sensitive to the Holy Spirit, God will always place a person in your path to tell you that what you are doing is wrong. I learned this from personal experience. Now, all I have to do is think of the groups Paul singled out in his writing (1 Corinthians 6:9–11). Then I don't even entertain the idea of going there. It is so transformative that I am left with no other alternative but to reset and turn my focus back to God with a penitent heart.

God's help is available to each of us, for we all sin in thought, in word, or in our actions every day. My prayer is that you may now take the time to confess your faults before God and discipline yourself to stop whatever foolishness you are doing. Get help if it is addiction, gambling, adultery, pornography—whatever it is. Yes, I am going to use this opportunity to encourage my colleagues. Nurses, we are some of the most caring people on the planet but we are not perfect people. If you have any dependency, stop what you are doing and get the help you need. Please.

We have a wonderful opportunity to ask our heavenly Father to forgive us; but once the breath of life leaves the body, that opportunity also expires. There is absolutely NO repentance in the grave. There is just no sugar-coating this stuff. These are the end days.

A person has only to take a moment to pause and to reflect on some of the dumb decisions made throughout his or her lifetime. If there is honest remorse, there is no better time to earnestly ask God's forgiveness of your errors and to invite him to come into your heart and life. It is as simple as this supporting evidence:

"All have sinned and come short of the glory of God" (Romans 3:23). The penalty for sin is death, from Adam to the last prophet.

The penalty for sin (past, present, and future) is death. "For the wages of sin is death: but the gift of God is eternal life through Christ Jesus our Lord" (Romans 6:23). You and I have to make an informed decision to stop serving the thing, the person, the habit that drives every moment of every day of our lives in such an unorthodox way that it becomes self-serving.

This can be any vice, from an obsession with technology to unhealthy behaviors like adultery, money laundering, murder, trafficking, lying, or manipulating. Paul heaped them all into one large group in 1 Corinthians 6:10. Paul called them the unrighteous ... but so are many of us.

"For sin shall not have dominion over us: For you are no longer governed by sin but by the redemptive grace of our Lord and Savior Jesus Christ (Romans 6:14). The entire book of Romas merits reading in your spare time. It will help you confirm who really has dominion over your life—not the old master, who would drag you further into the quagmire of life but One who would keep extending a hand to pull you out of the quagmire you are sitting in right now.

"Herein is love, not that we loved God, but that he loved us, and sent his Son to be the propitiation for our sin" (1 John 4:10). Propitiation purely means Jesus Christ paid the penalty for sin. The Apostle John continually reminds us of Christ's everlasting love: For God so loved the world that He gave His son's life in place of yours. This is one time you can feel narcissistic because you mean that much to Him. Isn't it amazing that it does not matter where you come from or how far off you have wandered from God? John 3:16 is one passage of Scripture that will leap back to your memory the moment you open your heart to Jesus Christ. He came, he lived, he died, and he is still alive in our hearts. This will be the theme of Luke's gospel. Let it be the theme of your life also. "Now, the

God of hope fill you with all joy and peace in believing, that ye may abound in hope, through the power of the Holy Ghost" (Romans 15:13).

What then, one might ask, can we do on the Sabbath? Rest. Everybody plans ahead when they are going on a vacation—choosing the departure date, packing suitable clothes for the weather changes, estimating the cost for food and beverage, transportation, and tours. Why not take the same approach and plan for your workweek? Plan the meals, the commute time (give or take traffic) and the podcasts you will listen to during that time, your appointments, bedtimes, and most importantly, when you will spend some time with the person who woke you up this morning. I am going to be blatantly honest here. For most of my adult life my definition of "rest" was this: Rest was a change of occupation. Thankfully, the nursing profession is so broad that I could switch from one area of service to another without changing occupations. I moved through like a professor who wanted to be an expert in every area: psychiatry, medical/surgical, pediatrics, labor and delivery, neonatal, obstetrics and gynecology, neuro, public health, hospice—caring for others from the womb to the tomb.

I believe we are living in a time when people like honesty, for the most part. I am literally editing my book after my initial publication on December 25, 2024. Here, I am giving my readers an honest glimpse of why writing is such a challenge for me. I want to abbreviate every word, shorten every sentence, leave out the subjects, and overwhelm you with run-on sentences. Just give me a break with this one. Let it be a medical-surgical benchmark for improvement as you take this writing journey with me. Rest assured.

Rest assured the Sabbath is still a perfect day to witness to others, show compassion and kindness, visit the sick and shut-in, share a meal with widows and neighbors, and feed the homeless in our respective communities. One might argue that all of the above is work. This supports my argument that rest is just a change from the gruesome noise of the everyday grind of life to a realignment with the things of God. In doing the latter, your stress level decreases, your priorities shift, and you fill the gaps of isolation with socialization and create space for longevity. When you perform one random act of kindness for the day, you can put your feet up and take a nap. I promise you this sleep will be much sweeter than the sleep after coming home tired from eight or twelve hours of hitting the ground running and no time to eat or empty your bladder. It's sweat equity (Genesis 3:19). The reality is that life is a balancing act of faith and work. "For as the body without the spirit is dead, so faith without works is dead also." (James 2:26).

The Second Chapter of Luke's Gospel

1 And it came to pass in those days, that there went out a decree from Caesar Augustus that all the world should be taxed.

2 (And this taxing was first made when Cyrenius was governor of Syria.)

3 And all went to be taxed, everyone into his own city.

4 And Joseph also went up from Galilee, out of the city of Nazareth, into Judaea, unto the city of David, which is called Bethlehem; (because he was of the house and lineage of David:)

5 To be taxed with Mary, his espoused wife, being great with child.

6 And so it was, that, while they were there, the days were accomplished that she should be delivered.

7 And she brought forth her firstborn son, and wrapped him in swaddling clothes, and laid him in a manger, because there was no room for them in the inn.

8 And there were in the same country shepherds abiding in the field, keeping watch over their flock by night.

9 And, lo, the angel of the Lord came upon them, and the glory of the Lord shone round about them: and they were sore afraid.

10 And the angel said unto them, Fear not: for, behold, I bring you good tidings of great joy, which shall be to all people.

11 For unto you is born this day in the city of David a Savior, which is Christ the Lord.

12 And this shall be a sign unto you; Ye shall find the babe wrapped in swaddling clothes, lying in a manger.

13 And suddenly there was with the angel a multitude of the heavenly host praising God, and saying,

14 Glory to God in the highest, and on earth peace, good will toward men.

15 And it came to pass, as the angels were gone away from them into heaven, the shepherds said one to another, Let us now go even unto Bethlehem, and see this thing, which is come to pass, which the Lord hath made known unto us.

16 And they came with haste, and found Mary, and Joseph, and the babe lying in a manger.

17 And when they had seen it, they made known abroad the saying which was told them concerning this child.

18 And all they that heard it wondered at those things which were told them by the shepherds.

19 But Mary kept all these things and pondered them in her heart.

20 And the shepherds returned, glorifying and praising God for all the things that they had heard and seen, as it was told unto them.

21 And when eight days were accomplished for the circumcising of the child, his name was called JESUS, which was so named of the angel before he was conceived in the womb.

22 And when the days of her purification according to the law of Moses were accomplished, they brought him to Jerusalem, to present him to the Lord.

23 (As it is written in the law of the LORD, Every male that openeth the womb shall be called holy to the Lord;)

24 And to offer a sacrifice according to that which is said in the law of the Lord, A pair of turtledoves, or two young pigeons.

25 And, behold, there was a man in Jerusalem, whose name was Simeon; and the same man was just and devout, waiting for the consolation of Israel: and the Holy Ghost was upon him.

26 And it was revealed unto him by the Holy Ghost, that he should not see death, before he had seen the Lord's Christ.

27 And he came by the Spirit into the temple: and when the parents brought in the child Jesus, to do for him after the custom of the law,

28 Then took he him up in his arms, and blessed God, and said,

29 Lord, now lettest thou thy servant depart in peace, according to thy word:

30 For mine eyes have seen thy salvation,

31 Which thou hast prepared before the face of all people;

32 A light to lighten the Gentiles, and the glory of thy people Israel.

33 And Joseph and his mother marveled at those things which were spoken of him.

34 And Simeon blessed them, and said unto Mary his mother, Behold, this child is set for the fall and rising again of many in Israel; and for a sign which shall be spoken against.

35 (Yea, a sword shall pierce through thy own soul also,) that the thoughts of many hearts may be revealed.

36 And there was one Anna, a prophetess, the daughter of Phanuel, of the tribe of Aser: she was of a great age, and had lived with an husband seven years from her virginity;

37 And she was a widow of about fourscore and four years, which departed not from the temple, but served God with fastings and prayers night and day.

38 And she coming in that instant gave thanks likewise unto the Lord, and spake of him to all them that looked for redemption in Jerusalem.

39 And when they had performed all things according to the law of the Lord, they returned into Galilee, to their own city Nazareth.

40 And the child grew, and waxed strong in spirit, filled with wisdom: and the grace of God was upon him.

41 Now his parents went to Jerusalem every year at the feast of the Passover.

42 And when he was twelve years old, they went up to Jerusalem after the custom of the feast.

43 And when they had fulfilled the days, as they returned, the child Jesus tarried behind in Jerusalem; and Joseph and his mother knew not of it.

44 But they, supposing him to have been in the company, went a day's journey; and they sought him among their kinsfolk and acquaintance.

45 And when they found him not, they turned back again to Jerusalem, seeking him.

46 And it came to pass, that after three days they found him in the temple, sitting in the midst of the doctors, both hearing them, and asking them questions.

47 And all that heard him were astonished at his understanding and answers.

48 And when they saw him, they were amazed: and his mother said unto him, Son, why hast thou thus dealt with us? behold, thy Father and I have sought thee sorrowing.

49 And he said unto them, How is it that ye sought me? wist ye not that I must be about my Father's business?

50 And they understood not the saying which he spake unto them.

51 And he went down with them, and came to Nazareth, and was subject unto them: but his mother kept all these sayings in her heart.

52 And Jesus increased in wisdom and stature, and in favor with God and man.

King James Version (KJV, public domain)

Chapter 2

The division of Levites: A firm foundation

Here is a brief synopsis of the backstory on the priesthood. I gleaned most of it from the first book of the Chronicles.

David had become frail and was in his last years as king, so he officially appointed his son Solomon to reign as co-regent. King David loved to worship God; because of his adoration, David wanted the temple to be accessible for worship day and night. To fulfill all the duties involved in maintaining the temple—the order of services, the animal sacrifices, the instruments, and musicians for every service—the king needed as many descendants of the priesthood as he could find. First David summoned the Levites. Keep in mind that, in the time of Moses, God had appointed only Aaron as priest because he was a direct descendant of Levi, one of Jacob's twelve sons.

Strong's *Concordance* gives the epistemology of the Hebrew word *Levi* (# 38881), which is related to the verb *Lavah* that means "to join." The Levites were the picture of God's covenant or joint relationship with mankind. God made a covenant with Moses; this is commonly known as the Mosaic Covenant, but God did not decree that Moses's boys were to assume positions or perform duties as priests. Only Aaron and his descendants could enter the Levitical (derived from the book of laws/ Leviticus and the Levi) priesthood at the very outset. They had to be twenty years or older (Numbers 8:24–25). Aaron had four boys: Nadab, Abihu, Eleazar, and Ithmar. Nadab and Abihu died leaving Eleazar and Ithmar.

By the time David decided to recruit priests for temple work, Eleazar's priestly offspring were Zadok and his sons. Eleazar's brother was Ithmar, whose descendants included the priest Ahimelech. David was able to gather sixteen groups of workers from Eleazar's larger family and eight groups from Ahimelech's smaller family for a total of twenty-four groups of temple workers. According to tradition, they could not enter the priesthood until age twenty-five and they had to retire at age fifty (Numbers 8:24–25). David would change this requirement.

Among other rules, they would cast lots for their position (1 Chronicles 25:8). This practice of decision making continued more than one thousand years. Bible scholars subtracted the midpoint of David's reign (990 BC) from the time of Jesus's birth around 4 BC to give lay readers a general idea how long these practices continued. Zacharias was still casting lots and hoping for his desired position (Luke 1:9). Amazing! I am blown away by the scholars who painstakingly correlated Jewish, Greek, Roman events, and combined these with astrology to get these dates. Now we have all this information at our fingertips. I am so grateful. The risk we take in making any literary work public is that of human error; and that, my friends, defines the word "bravery." With all of that aside, I still had a difficult time following David's merger with the sons of Levi.

The sons of Levi were Gershon, Kohath, and Merari (Exodus 6:16). The sons of Merari were Mushi, Mahli and Jaaziah (1 Chronicles 23:23). The sons of Mahli were Eleazar and Kish. Eleazar had died without having any sons, but he had daughters. Kish, the surviving brother, gave permission for the girls to marry their cousins, which was customary in those days. Check out the backstory on how David would benefit from this merger.

King David's pride was in the strength of his army. This was his hubris. He could have been a good Certified Public Accountant. He would take a census of his army at least twice during his reign. The first was incited by Satan when he stood against Israel as recorded in 1 Chronicles 21:1–4. The second time is reported: "And again the anger of the Lord was kindled against Israel, and he moved David against them to say, Go number Israel and Judah" (2 Samuel 24:1–2). Joab was a very insightful captain of the Lord's army. The king gave him the order "Go now through all the tribes of Israel, from Dan to Beersheba and number ye the people, that I may know the number of the people."

Joab wisely and politely responded to his commander in chief: "Now the Lord thy God add unto the people, how many soever they be, an hundredfold, and that the eyes of lord the king may see it: but why doth my lord the king delight in this thing?" (1 Chronicles 21:1–3). David ignored the advice of the captain of his army and went on and took the census anyway.

God would punish David. I believe David journaled his error and later published it in the thirty–third psalm (Psalm 33:16).

His hubris became his hamartia. Having learned his lesson, the king did not take a census this time. Instead, he did two things.

First, he lowered the age to enter the Levitical priesthood from twenty-five years according to the law given to Moses. The king counted them off from thirty years and above but he would later lower the age of admission from twenty-five to twenty years old (1 Chronicles 23:27). In lowering the age of admission, he would get more applicants for ministry roles, and he had many to fill. David recruited more than 38,000 temple workers and that number was still inadequate to carry out all the work required to prepare for feast days, Sabbaths, new moons, and burnt offerings. David had to have enough priests to serve. He also needed to rotate the shifts more fairly and to cover all the ministerial duties associated with these elaborate services (1 Chronicles 23:28–32).

Keep in mind that King David had taken on all of this in his old age. The temple had not yet been built but he had a clear vision of what he wanted these services to look like within the temple. The tabernacle would no longer have to be constantly carried from place to place and neither would poles have to be torn down and rebuilt at every destination where they camped. Since God had not given the king his stamp of approval to build His temple, David felt a sense of urgency to do the preparation for it.

During this time, the tabernacle was temporarily housed at Gibeon, Mount Zion, but David nurtured a deep desire to build a permanent place for the ark of the covenant. Nathan, the prophet, told him God had pretty much said, *That was a great idea, but your son Solomon will build the temple* (my paraphrase). I can only imagine how disappointed the king was, but he never argued with God. Instead, he made his son Solomon the king and David handed off the blueprint for the building to him instead of getting anxious or going into a depressive mood about it. Knowing David's persistent character, he likely went back to God and said *I can't just sit here and do nothing, You know that, Lord! So, what do you want me to do instead?* God gave him the vision and he would have his scribes chronicle every detail of his achievements. David not only lowered the age of admission to the priesthood, but he also expanded the number of divisions. These are the twenty-four divisions that Luke alludes to in his gospel.

The Levitical priesthood had twenty-two shifts, which consisted of nine Gershonite, nine Kohathite, and four Merarite. How did David add two more divisions that Luke would include in his research? David expanded the priesthood by merging the progeny of Levi's sons, Merari, Eleazar, and Kish. Eleazar had only daughters who married sons of their cousin, Kish. This merger between Mahli's two bloodlines formed one division of the priesthood. During King David's search for additional temple workers, he ordered the priest to document all the priests within the lineage of Jacob's twelve sons. God called the tribe of Levi to the priesthood.

Levites were the only priests given God's authority to enter the Holy of Holies. David separated these priests for this singular assignment according to the tradition and kept those ordinances carefully. In his search, the king ordered Shemaiah to write down the names according to their descendants of families and to only cast lots for their shifts or the rotation of duties. Shemaiah was documenting the priestly line of the sons of Aaron, Moses's brother, when he identified Abijah. The lot fell on Abijah for rotation within the eighth division (1 Chronicles 24:10).

This is how far back Luke went to establish the descendants of his main players in the story of Jesus. Indeed, Zacharias was a descendant of Abijah and remained true to his traditions, living a righteous and set-apart life, HOLY, unto the Lord. Is there little wonder he was chosen? "A certain priest named Zacharias" (Luke 1:5) kept the law faithfully and lived a righteous life with his wife, Elisabeth. Their lives were a testament to this passage of Scriptures: "Godliness with contentment is a great gain" (1 Timothy 6:6). But Elisabeth was more than Zacharias's wife.

Introduction of Elisabeth

WHO WAS ELISABETH? Elisabeth was one of the triad of women whose faith Luke would masterfully use to establish the words spoken by the old prophets that Messiah would come. Elisabeth was a relative of Mary; they were first cousins, as the Angel Gabriel declared. Luke's gospel explains that Elisabeth, as Zachariah's wife, was barren and did not anticipate having children as she was well past childbearing age. Our twenty-first-century obstetricians would classify her as high risk. Even if she still had her uterus, she would not have been able to carry the baby to term, and in vitro fertilization was out of the question. Elisabeth's entire scenario involved just too much risk. She would have been encouraged to abort little John and save her life. Only good old Hebrew midwives like Puah and Shiphrah could chance taking on this risky home delivery (Exodus 1:15–21).

But Elisabeth had gained a life of favor in the sight of the Lord because she strived to do what was right and pleasing to her Lord. There is little wonder why, as Elisabeth approached her third trimester, the Angel visited Mary, her cousin, and sent her to stay with Elisabeth. As I study this, I magnify the Holy Spirit with a smile on my face. I have always thought this trip was more for Mary. Perhaps its purpose was to conceal her from the public as she tried her best to grasp the magnitude of her immaculate conception. What would she say to her fiancé Joseph, not to mention her parents! But the Holy Spirit revealed that this visit was also for Elisabeth. Women need the support of other women, especially during the birthing process in a time when men are allowed nowhere near the Red Tent. I believe that Mary stayed with Elisabeth and held her hand, breathed with her, repositioned her, and helped her until baby John poked his little head into the world.

Zacharias, Elisabeth's husband, had demonstrated a little less faith, and for that he remained speechless throughout all of his wife's pregnancy.

Who was Mary?

THIS IS A PERFECT PLACE to introduce the young virgin whom God hand-picked to present himself to the world in human form. Elisabeth's pregnancy had resulted from Zacharias's expectancy to have a child. They had read about Abe and Sarah's wavering faith and about Rachel, Hannah, and other women who all had reproductive issues. Some scholars will argue that Joseph was an older man and could have easily fallen into that infertility category, but I beg to differ. I would like to think that, even if he were an "older man," he would be in his early twenties, and Mary had just turned thirteen. As they say these days, age is just a number. Joseph demonstrated his love for her and was very protective of her. There is no mention of abuse. His love for his trade as a carpenter made him a good provider for his family. He was a devout man who was faithful to his wife and his family.

Mary, like Zacharias, was afraid. Who would not be if an Angel of God appeared and announced, "Hail, thou that art highly favoured, the Lord is with thee" (Luke 1:28). A jolt like that, even if in a dream, would bring quick repentance for the faint of heart. We can be thankful that God taught his angels how to perform cardiopulmonary resuscitation (CPR). If a messenger is of God, all he has to do is say, "Do not be afraid" and everything returns to perfect homeostasis. The angel continued "Rejoice highly favored one, the Lord is with you; blessed are you among women!" (Luke 1:28).

Throughout Luke's record, you will notice the prominence he gives to the Holy Spirit. Mary should have been shaking like a leaf but she did not flinch. Instead, she bravely asked Gabriel the hard question. Her response to the Angel, "How can these things be, since I do not know a man?" implies that she was still a virgin.

"The Holy Spirit will come upon you, and the power of the Highest will overshadow you; therefore, the Holy one who is to be born will be called the son of God..." Then Gabriel told her about Elisabeth's pregnancy and that she was in her second trimester, and said Mary should go to Elisabeth right way. This is recorded in Luke 1:26–36.

Unlike Elisabeth's performance-based conception, Mary's conception was completely immaculate, an expression of God's sinless nature. It is an expression the world is still trying to wrap its head around.

A brilliance that is highly incompatible with science. Ouch! No wonder the Apostle John, in John 1:1, began his writings with "In the beginning was the Word, and the Word was with God, and the Word was God." A "punch in the throat," as Lisa Harper would say. John dismisses all heretical teaching that Jesus was "just another prophet" or "just another Greek or Hellenistic god" and that "he was not fully God." Every person is entitled to believe what they choose but, as Christ's followers, let us contend for the faith (Jude 1:3–5). Some Greek scholars go to the extreme of arguing that the Apostle John left out the article *ho*, which would have given the subject *Theos* (God) a title that should read in their language *Theos en ho logos*; but because it did not read like that, they interpreted it to mean Christ was just another minor god. Seriously!

A noteworthy observation is that John used the word "was" three times in the imperfect tense to describe the continuation of the existence of God. John said, away with your heretic practices for "All things were made through Him, (Genesis 1:1), and through God the SON all creation was made (Colossians 1:16; Hebrews 1:2). Ladies and gentlemen, rest assured that Jesus is God incarnate indeed. Luke settles the question of His deity once and for all.

In addition to Elisabeth and Mary, there was a third woman in the triad. Her name was Anna, and we meet her in Chapter 3.

The Third Chapter of Luke's Gospel

1 Now in the fifteenth year of the reign of Tiberius Caesar, Pontius Pilate being governor of Judaea, and Herod being tetrarch of Galilee, and his brother Philip tetrarch of Ituraea and of the region of Trachonitis, and Lysanias the tetrarch of Abilene,

2 Annas and Caiaphas being the high priests, the word of God came unto John the son of Zacharias in the wilderness.

3 And he came into all the country about Jordan, preaching the baptism of repentance for the remission of sins.

4 As it is written in the book of the words of Esaias the prophet, saying, The voice of one crying in the wilderness, Prepare ye the way of the Lord, make his paths straight.

5 Every valley shall be filled, and every mountain and hill shall be brought low; and the crooked shall be made straight, and the rough ways shall be made smooth;

6 And all flesh shall see the salvation of God.

7 Then said he to the multitude that came forth to be baptized of him, O generation of vipers, who hath warned you to flee from the wrath to come?

8 Bring forth therefore fruits worthy of repentance, and begin not to say within yourselves, We have Abraham to our father: for I say unto you, That God is able of these stones to raise up children unto Abraham.

9 And now also the axe is laid unto the root of the trees: every tree therefore which bringeth not forth good fruit is hewn down, and cast into the fire.

10 And the people asked him, saying, What shall we do then?

11 He answereth and saith unto them, He that hath two coats, let him impart to him that hath none; and he that hath meat, let him do likewise.

12 Then came also publicans to be baptized, and said unto him, Master, what shall we do?

13 And he said unto them, Exact no more than that which is appointed you.

14 And the soldiers likewise demanded of him, saying, And what shall we do? And he said unto them, Do violence to no man, neither accuse any falsely; and be content with your wages.

15 And as the people were in expectation, and all men mused in their hearts of John, whether he were the Christ, or not;

16 John answered, saying unto them all, I indeed baptize you with water; but one mightier than I cometh, the latchet of whose shoes I am not worthy to unloose: he shall baptize you with the Holy Ghost and with fire:

17 Whose fan is in his hand, and he will thoroughly purge his floor, and will gather the wheat into his garner; but the chaff he will burn with fire unquenchable.

18 And many other things in his exhortation preached he unto the people.

19 But Herod the tetrarch, being reproved by him for Herodias his brother Philip's wife, and for all the evils which Herod had done,

20 Added yet this above all, that he shut up John in prison.

21 Now when all the people were baptized, it came to pass, that Jesus also being baptized, and praying, the heaven was opened,

22 And the Holy Ghost descended in a bodily shape like a dove upon him, and a voice came from heaven, which said, Thou art my beloved Son; in thee I am well pleased.

23 And Jesus himself began to be about thirty years of age, being (as was supposed) the son of Joseph, which was the son of Heli,

24 Which was the son of Matthat, which was the son of Levi, which was the son of Melchi, which was the son of Janna, which was the son of Joseph,

25 Which was the son of Mattathias, which was the son of Amos, which was the son of Naum, which was the son of Esli, which was the son of Nagge,

26 Which was the son of Maath, which was the son of Mattathias, which was the son of Semei, which was the son of Joseph, which was the son of Juda,

27 Which was the son of Joanna, which was the son of Rhesa, which was the son of Zorobabel, which was the son of Salathiel, which was the son of Neri,

28 Which was the son of Melchi, which was the son of Addi, which was the son of Cosam, which was the son of Elmodam, which was the son of Er,

29 Which was the son of Jose, which was the son of Eliezer, which was the son of Jorim, which was the son of Matthat, which was the son of Levi.

30 Which was the son of Simeon, which was the son of Juda, which was the son of Joseph, which was the son of Jonan, which was the son of Eliakim,

31 Which was the son of Melea, which was the son of Menan, which was the son of Mattatha, which was the son of Nathan, which was the son of David,

32 Which was the son of Jesse, which was the son of Obed, which was the son of Booz, which was the son of Salmon, which was the son of Naasson,

33 Which was the son of Aminadab, which was the son of Aram, which was the son of Esrom, which was the son of Phares, which was the son of Juda,

34 Which was the son of Jacob, which was the son of Isaac, which was the son of Abraham, which was the son of Thara, which was the son of Nachor,

35 Which was the son of Saruch, which was the son of Ragau, which was the son of Phalec, which was the son of Heber, which was the son of Sala,

36 Which was the son of Cainan, which was the son of Arphaxad, which was the son of Sem, which was the son of Noe, which was the son of Lamech,

37 Which was the son of Mathusala, which was the son of Enoch, which was the son of Jared, which was the son of Maleleel, which was the son of Cainan,

38 Which was the son of Enos, which was the son of Seth, which was the son of Adam, which was the son of God.

King James Version (KJV, public domain)

Chapter 3

"And he shall be called John."

– Angel Gabriel (Luke 1:13)

Every year, 18,000 priests waited prayerfully for the high priests to cast lots to assign each to a service role, a customary Jewish practice (Joshua 18:6–10; 1 Chronicles 24:5–31; 2:8–9; 26:13–16). While waiting, Zacharias prayed for the most envied position, "his lot to burn incense," a once-in-a-lifetime opportunity. This event is held outside the church at the hour of prayer.

When he heard it had fallen on him to burn incense (Luke 1:9), Zach was excited because he would be standing in the holy place where the altar of incense was the only thing before the veil that separated him from entering the Holy of Holies. One pull of those curtains and Zacharias would be standing before the Ark of Testimony where the presence of God was (Exodus 25:22). He was deep in these thoughts when he heard the Angel Gabriel say, "Do not be afraid, Zacharias!" He was standing beside Zacharias at the altar of incense. "Your prayers have been heard, and your wife Elisabeth will bear you a son, and you shall call his name John" (Luke 1:13). Wow!

God heard Zacharias's prayers. Zacharias likely poured his heart out to God during the prayer time. He was not distracted by what was going on around him. He was told that his wife

Elisabeth would have a son. Elisabeth lived a virtuous life with her husband but could not have children. Like millions of women today, she probably suffered from endometriosis. But God, who predestined their lives, would cause them to conceive and give birth to a son whose destiny was to prepare the way for the Son of God. Their son would also go before HIM in the spirit and power of Elijah (Luke 1:17).

Many would rejoice at his birth, for:

- He will bring joy and gladness.
- He shall not drink wine or strong drink, a strict criterion of Hebrew tradition known as the Nazarite vow, a vow of separation. Read (Numbers 6:1–21).
- He will be filled with the Holy Spirit from His mother's womb. Bible scholars suggest John the Baptist had to be born filled with the Holy Spirit because he would be the one to baptize Jesus Christ (Luke 1:15).
- And he would also cause many of the children of Israel (Jews) to turn toward the Lord, their God.

I heard it rightly said that a text without a context is a pretext for a proof text, and it has become my rationale for my backstories in teaching. College students know that professors like to tell stories. Some like the stories but others find them unappealing. However, evaluations often reveal otherwise. When asked, How did you arrive at your answer to ...? the response often goes back to the moral of a story shared in class within the context of the problem discussed. Relativism. So, here is the backstory of Judah, relative to John, influencing Israel's belief in the Lord.

Extra! Extra! Read all about it: King Josiah is dead, and the King of Babylon is heading our way. Let us humble ourselves and submit to him, and perhaps God will relent, for we have sinned greatly against the Lord.

I imagine that was Jeremiah's cry for forty long years. The Southern Kingdom of Judah (two tribes) fell to the Babylonians around 604–538 BC or 586–587 BC. I like to refer to the latter because it is associated with rebuilding and rededicating the temple in Jerusalem. Those who managed to escape fled to the Northern Kingdom. The Northern Kingdom (ten tribes) later fell to the Assyrians in 722 BC.

Daniel was among the first in a series of Babylonian captives who never returned but remained in captivity for seventy years, as predicted by Jeremiah (Jeremiah 29:10; 2 Chronicles 36:20–21). King Cyrus gave the remaining Hebrew people (who were rebranded as Israelites after conquering the Canaanites) permission to return in 538 BC. This is the remnant of Israel now residing within the regions of the Roman Empire. These are the people whose hearts the Angel Gabriel told Zacharias that his son John would turn toward God in a ministry parallel to that of the prophet Elijah. It was Elijah who publicly confronted the prophets and priests of Baal on Mount Carmel (1 Kings 18:16–45). He also called out King Ahab and his wife, Jezebel, for their injustices to the poor, such as stealing Naboth's vineyard (1 Kings 21:1–16).

Similarly, John would preach repentance and the turning from sin, adding water baptism as the outward sign of inner conversion. John would speak out against the injustices and the unlawful marriage of Herod to his brother's wife, Herodias. The latter would cost John his life. This historical narrative is foundational to the story of the birth, life, and ministry of John the Baptist. Still, it would also be important to the redemptive work of Christ: his birth, life, death, burial, resurrection, and imminent return. Jesus would also allude to the prophet Elijah in his earthly ministry in Matthew 17:11–12.

One cannot help but wonder who, if any in our day, is marked as the figurative Elijah who outs injustices and mistreatment of the poor. We see the gap widening among people with little or no tolerance for differences. The economic gap widens every time the bell rings on the stock exchange floor. The poor are being turned away from hospitals for lack of insurance, while the rich increasingly seek treatment overseas. The real question is, How will we know when we, the church, are so divided?

Zacharias spent all his life in church looking for a savior, and he did not recognize the messenger of God (Luke 1:11–13). We can safely assume it was at least nine months until John was born, as that is the usual length of pregnancy.

Six months after Elisabeth conceived, the angel messenger, Gabriel, made another trip to earth, this time to a young virgin named Mary. Luke, who had graduated magna cum laude from St. Paul's University of Apostleship, had mastered the art of inspired storytelling and decided he would not copy Matt's gospel.

Luke is different. No doubt. While Matthew narrates his story from Joseph's perspective, Luke shares the announcement from Mary's point of view. Again, Luke returns to the ancient story of Abraham, Sarah, and Hagar. Abe's wife, Sarah, had become aggravated by the behavior of Hagar who was pregnant with her husband's child. This was not in vitro, so Hagar was getting a bit testy with her mistress. Sarah became jealous despite her good intentions, for it was her idea to help God (as we often do in our sinful state) by providing a woman for her husband. Abe's response to his wife prompts me to look at Adam's response to God when he was confronted after eating the fruit his wife gave him from the tree of good and evil, saying, "It's the woman thou gavest me" (Genesis 3:12).

Abe did no such thing. Like Adam he could have said, "It is that woman you gave to me" but he did not. Instead, he calmly told his wife, *It is your decision. Do as you please.* Abe's response tells me he was indifferent to her youth and to the propensity to start a harem, or he had let his desires run amok.

Did you not think this thing all the way through before you sent her to my bed? Sarah was likely suffering from endometriosis and Abe from erectile dysfunction, so he did not care one way or the other. He knew God would have to perform a reproductive miracle in both bodies. Seemingly, reproductive issues were common in ancient times, especially among women. One wonders if the early onset of marriage at age twelve or thirteen played a role as this tradition is the common denominator in Sarah, Rachel, and Hannah and would also impact Elisabeth.

Nevertheless, Sarah's attempt to resolve her barrenness by proxy backfired as Genesis 16:6 tells us that Sarah dealt so harshly with her that the damsel ran away.

This is the humiliating position Hagar was in, sitting by a brook, all forlorn and perhaps remorseful that her devotion and obedience to her mistress had led to her situation. Likely she asked herself, *Why did I not run away in the first place? I have no place to go, and no one will love me now that my reputation is tarnished.* This is the Hagar's posture when the angel of the Lord finds her. He speaks directly to her and tells her what to do and what the future of her unborn child will be. What a comfort we have in Jesus even when we are damaged. God still hears. Hagar would be obedient and returned to her mistress; she would give birth to a nation through her son, Ishmael, just as God promised. The problem began when God rejected Ishmael and chose the child of promise, Isaac, to birth the nation of Israel. This would result in a conflict that continues up until today.

A Gentile himself, Luke knew firsthand how first-century society treated women. He had to explore how twelve-year-old Mary, who was already engaged to an older dude named Joseph, would fare under Sharia law. First-century Jews touted that they would rather the Torah be burned than be read by a woman. The world must know her side of the story. Luke would show how a merciful, kind, and loving God would take the outliers of society and not glorify their sin but make them heroines of FAITH. Unfortunately, the treatment of women remains marginalized in many parts of the world today.

Even more unfortunate is the continuation of this treatment of women in the church. The Corinthian converts were largely of pagan background. It is within that context that the Apostle Paul confronted their behaviors. The Apostle Paul did "silence" those feline, disruptive chatterboxes upstairs at the First Church of Corinth Justified (1 Corinthians 14:34). His reprimand can be paraphrased as, *Discuss this at home around the dinner table with your husband.*

The Corinthian church was hell on wheels, as evidenced by their obnoxious behaviors: misusing communion, incest, eating foods offered to idols, being in church on Sundays but participating in pagan worship on Mondays. This church was over the top; they were used to idols who could not talk back, but now they were learning about gifts (Greek: *charismata*) and seeing these gifts in operation. Now I see the origin of the Charismatic, a "gift"-oriented movement in the 1960s and 1970s. Every movement has some good but, like the human body, no one member can function as "all-seeing" and "all-knowing"; the pancreas will never carry out the functions of the liver, nor will the hand do as well as intended if it were to become a prosthetic foot.

The church is to function as one body even though every member has a different function. This takes your whole life. Now stop and take a few minutes to pray earnestly for your pastor, his family, and the leadership of your local assembly, for they have a tough job if you and I are members. My only saving grace is to stay in the Word of God. What is yours? Do you understand why the Apostle Paul rightly used the Corinthian church as the conscience for other New Testament churches in Asia Minor?

These examples were carefully written and preserved for our learning, not to isolate women from worship or to shame them publicly as some men do. Only a few verses prior (1 Corinthians 11:4), the Apostle commended women for praying with their heads covered as a sign of honor to their husbands. Is he bipolar? Absolutely not! Paul admonishes believers to take advantage of the liberty wherein Christ has made us free. We all have the power to choose, but God's grace works in our hearts daily to constrain us from usurping authority over our men. In that light, I don't want to be beaten over the head with it and be used as collateral damage for Eve's disobedience to her husband. The idolatrous talking snake lied to her with his sneaky self, sprawled all over the tree, touching the very forbidden saying, "Yea, hath God said, ye shall not eat of every tree of the garden?" (Genesis 2:16–17).

"And the woman said unto the serpent, We may eat of the fruit of the trees of the garden: But of the fruit of the tree, which is in the midst of the garden, God hath said, Ye shall not eat of it, **neither shall ye touch it**, lest ye die."

Seriously! Did God say that, or did Adam add that in his warning to Eve to stress the importance of staying away from the darn tree? Thanks, Adam and Eve. You are both responsible, sir. Adam's response could have been, *Honey, where did you get that from?* (Dear God, I hope she would be honest, but we all have sinned and come short of the glory of God.) And if she were honest, he would likely have responded,

NO, thanks. God distinctly said we must not eat of it. And I asked you not even to go close enough to touch it. Admittedly, I am taking some liberty here in paraphrasing the scenario.

Let me use a more modern example of the power of influence. Take my friends, G and R, who are two beautiful people and an awesome Christian couple. Before the availability of GPS, R would sometimes get turned around while driving on unfamiliar streets. G would say, "Honey, you need to turn down this street. Just make a left here and get back on Avenue Z."

R would unquestioningly obey his sweetheart. Days later he would laughingly tell the story. "I was so lost last night. I knew I should have made a right turn on Bright Street, but when my wife tells me, 'Honey, you need to turn here.' I don't think—I just make the turn."

Over time, R learned to take his rightful position in the relationship in a very loving way and asked more probing questions together. They would either agree or agree to disagree, but they never cast blame or point fingers at each other. The end game is this: Just as the omnipotent God had a special plan for women in Eve's fall from grace, He also had place for women in his redemptive plan through Mary. All through Scriptures we can trace examples of the women he nominated to be in his lineage. It is a record of his grace and mercy. What could be more encouraging than the story of the Canaanite woman, Rahab, in Joshua 2:1–21?

Chapter 4

The Birth of Jesus

Luke, Chapter Two, begins: "And it came to pass in those days, that there went out a decree from Caesar Augustus that all the world should be taxed" (Luke 2:1).

Augustus was Roman Emperor from 31 BC to 14 AD. He was born Gaius Octavius Caepias (63 BC–AD 14). His predecessor was his great-uncle Julius Caesar, who adopted him as his own son because he no longer had a living heir after his daughter's died in childbirth ("Augustus [63 BC–AD 14]," BBC History 2014).

Julius favored the Jews who had occupied Alexandria and then Rome for over 2,000 years. He instituted laws to support their assimilation throughout their diaspora, which began with the Assyrian conquest of southern Judah and was later followed by the Babylonians of northern Jerusalem. The Jewish nation held a premise that one day God would unite them again, as the prophets had foretold: "For one day I will take you from among the heathen, and gather you out of all the countries, and will bring you back into your own land" (Ezekiel 36:24).

Gaius Octavius Caesar established Rome as an empire and instituted citizen registration for taxation. However, taxation was nothing new to the Jews, for it had already been instituted by Cyrenius, governor of Syria. "And all went to be taxed, everyone into his own city. And Joseph also went up from Galilee, out of the city of Nazareth, into Judea, unto the city of David, which is called Bethlehem: because he was of the house and lineage of David. To be taxed with Mary his espoused wife being great with child" (Luke 2:3–5).

This is the fulfillment of prophecy as spoken by the prophet Micah that the One who is to come would be born in Bethlehem:

But thou, Bethlehem Ephratah, though thou be little among the thousands of Judah, yet out of thee shall he come forth unto me that is to be ruler in Israel; whose going forth have been from of old, from everlasting" (Micah 5:2).

It would not matter, their existence in a pagan society, nor their circumstances, nor the stage of Mary's pregnancy. Mary would remain a virgin until three months after the birth of her baby, according to Mosaic law concerning purification after childbirth. Then they would have a huge marriage celebration according to their custom, and Joseph would consummate his marriage to Mary.

The Apostle Matthew implied that Joseph did the honorable thing and married Mary as soon as their engagement was publicized (Matthew 1:19). Becoming the human shield for his wife and her son, Joseph made a personal investment in the life of the woman he loved. Any lingering doubt Joseph may have entertained was put to rest when God spoke to him in a dream, saying, "Joseph, son of David, do not be afraid to take to you Mary your wife, for that which is conceived in her is of the Holy Spirit" (Matthew 1:20).

The thought of this kind of protection makes the arrector pili muscles raise the hair on my arms in gratitude to the mighty God I serve. Only God can turn the hearts of men to build a wall of protection around women. Lord, what will we do when they relentlessly strive to be us? God will have to come down again to fix another human dilemma. Oh Boy! In the meantime, we are not without hope.

Luke read Matthews's script and agreed that Joseph had married Mary sometime after he had been visited by God's messenger, Gabriel.

"Joseph also went up from Galilee, out of the city of Nazareth, into Judea, to the city of David, which is called Bethlehem because he was of the lineage of David, to be registered with Mary, his betrothed wife who was with child" (Luke 2:4–5). Mary and Joseph went up together to register his household, not just because they would be a family. They were both also ascribed to the tribe of Judah, Mary on her paternal side, and were established in the royal line of King David.

Chapter 5

The Herod Family

This is a historical introduction of territorial leaders within the Roman Empire in AD 27–29. Why? To establish irrefutable dates and times. "Now in the fifteenth year of the reign of Tiberius Caesar, Pontius Pilate being governor of Judea, Herod being the tetrarch of Galilee, his brother Philip tetrarch of Iturea and the region of Trachonitis, and Lysanias tetrarch of Abilene, while Annas and Caiaphas were high priests" (Luke 3:1–2).

As a prisoner of war, first-century writer Flavius Josephus, a former governor of Galilee, documented the backstories of these leaders extensively. Here is a brief synopsis of the trio of tetrarchs: Herod, Philip, and Lysanias. They were a force to be reckoned with because they were notorious for being mean, evil, and territorial.

The high priests were Caiphas and Annas, his father in- law. Both wielded more influence within the priesthood. This explains how the priests could easily get caught up in the politics of their day to the point where political issues began to inform their decisions. These are not new ideologies. Corruption was as rampant among the leaders then as it is now. King Solomon reminded us that there was nothing new under the sun (Ecclesiastes 1:9).

With the confusion and chaos facing the nation, John the Baptist would emerge from the wilderness, an uncultivated place, to baptize Jesus and introduce him to the world. This is John, the promised son of Zacharias and Elisabeth, now a grown man. He is depicted as a ruddy and handsome man with a lengthy overgrowth of hair everywhere—head, beard, arms, and legs—and with only a loin cloth for covering. What had happened to Johnny Boy? Was this the same kid who learned all the law and traditions from his dad? If he was anything like a young man I know with the same name, he would quip back: *My father did instruct me in the Torah, which also teaches that if a man is to receive the gift of the Torah, he must first make himself a wilderness.* This means to be in a state of openness and receptivity, like a wilderness.

For John to have survived in the physical sense, he had to rely completely on God for his protection as referenced in Genesis 21:14; Exodus 13:18, 15:22, and 17:1; Deuteronomy 2:8; Judges 1:16; Samuel 23:14, 23:24, and 24:1; Chronicles 20:16, 20:20; Psalms 29:8; Isaiah 21:1; and Mathew 3:1,3. Jesus would follow the same tradition, going off to his deserted place, referred to as *midbar* in the Hebrew Bible, where he would hear the voice of His.

There has to a separation in the life of a person who accepts the call to follow Christ. These men were intentional about their time of separation, and so must we be. Their emergence from the wilderness meant they had accepted their fate and were prepared to go off on the hero's journey. They would face immense challenges, get help from others, entertain doubt at times, and ultimately accept their fate.

Matthew traced Jesus's lineage all the way back to Abraham through his paternal side. Perhaps when Luke became it crystal clear that Jesus, the Messiah, was of the line of David (Matthew 1:1). With this proof on record, Jesus is the repairer of the breach (Isaiah 58:12) and is the only one who is eligible to sit on the throne of David and reign as king. Jesus, as the Godman, repairs the breaches between King David and his son King Solomon, between Israel and Judah; between Israel and Palestine, between North and South Korea, between the East and the West, the North and the South, and the everlasting gap between heaven and earth. He reigns as King of Kings forever and ever. Hallelujah!

Matthew traced the genealogy of Jesus from the paternal side, beginning with King David. In contrast, Luke traced it all the way back to Adam through his maternal side; he did not stop with David but went all the way back to Adam.

23 And Jesus Himself had become about thirty years of age, being (as was supposed) the son of Joseph, who was the son of Heli,

24 who was the son of Matthat, who was the son of Levi, who was the son of Melchi, who was the son of Janna, who was the son of Joseph,

25 who was the son of Mattathias, who was the son of Amos, who was the son of Nahum, who was the son of Esli, who was the son of Naggai,

26 who was the son of Maath, who was the son of Mattathias, who was the son of Semei, who was the son of Joseph, who was the son of Juda,

27 who was the son of Joanna, who was the son of Rhesa, who was the son of Zerubbabel, who was the son of Shealtiel, who was the son of Neri,

28 who was the son of Melchi, who was the son of Addi, who was the son of Cosam, who was the son of Elmodam, who was the son of Er,

29 who was the son of Jose, who was the son of Eliezer, who was the son of Jorim, who was the son of Matthat, who was the son of Levi,

30 who was the son of Simeon, who was the son of Judah, who was the son of Joseph, who was the son of Jonan, who was the son of Eliakim,

31 who was the son of Melea, who was the son of Menan, who was the son of Mattatha, who was the son of Nathan, who was the son of David,

32 who was the son of Jesse, who was the son of Obed, who was the son of Boaz, who was the son of Salmon, who was the son of Nahshon,

33 who was the son of Amminadab, who was the son of Aram, who was the son of Hezron, who was the son of Perez, who was the son of Judah,

34 who was the son of Jacob, who was the son of Isaac, who was the son of Abraham, who was the son of Terah, who was the son of Nahor,

35 who was the son of Serug, who was the son of Reu, who was the son of Peleg, who was the son of Eber, who was the son of Shelah,

36 who was the son of Cainan, who was the son of Arphaxad, who was the son of Shem, who was the son of Noah, who was the son of Lamech,

37 who was the son of Methuselah, who was the son of Enoch, who was the son of Jared, who was the son of Mahalaleel, who was the son of Cainan,

38 who was the son of Enos, who was the son of Seth, who was the son of Adam, who was the son of God.

(Luke 3:23–38)

Luke, as a Gentile Christian, was not steeped in ancient Hebrew customs. Therefore, he opted not to use the same discourse that Matthew had to establish Jesus as royalty and the rightful heir to the throne of God. Luke had read in the

Hebrew Talmud about all the treachery royalty brings. Was it not Absolom who tried to usurp his father's throne? (2 Samuel 15:1–18), not to mention the conspiracy of Shallum; are they not written in the book of the Chronicles? And Menahem, the son of Gadi, went up from Tirzah and smote Shallum, son of Jabesh, in Samaria, taking the throne by force (2 Kings 15:14).

Luke felt a deep need to prove that Jesus is not only the King of Kings but that He is Lord of Lords! He is most intentional about it. Jesus is the lord of the human heart. Both Matthew and Luke have left us a brilliant example of God's sovereignty. God used two men from different backgrounds and perspectives with the same intrinsic values and minds to accomplish his purpose.

Chapter 6

Shepherds still seek him

Luke interviews his first witnesses to the birth of Jesus Christ, shepherds who were outside the city limits. They were in another country, watching their flock out in the field. Although he did not repeat the scenario with the wise men, he chose to travel over rough terrain and through the countryside to interview people who knew the shepherds' story. Shepherds were considered outcasts, the dregs of society. I greatly appreciate how Luke included more of society's marginal people in his narrative than Mathew did. Here is an example that stood out for me.

Quickly flip back to Matthew, then notice how Luke gives us a different perspective on visitors from the Middle East. Matthew's first witnesses were the wise men (Magi) who stopped by the palace first to pay homage to the king and to get his permission to knock on doors, as was their prestigious custom. According to astronomy professor Craig Chester with the Monterey Institute for Research in Astronomy, these men were likely either Arab Jews who were among the scattered remnant, Zoroastrians, Medes, or Persians.

The word *magi* is Greek and was ascribed only to priestly men who would proclaim the signs of the times and their interpretations of them. Daniel was one such person and was recognized as chief magus to King Nebuchadnezzar's court

(Daniel 5:11). Daniel also documented his visions in the book bearing his name, which was likely read by magicians like these hundreds of years before Jesus's star appeared. They, too, anticipated the arrival of a king. The magi's arrival in Bethlehem dismissed any sense of timing as they reached Bethlehem one year later. One can only suppose the reason is that it took this time to travel on foot the nine hundred miles from Baghdad in Iraq to Bethlehem in Judah.

Luke's perspective gives us a sense of urgency. When Mary gave birth in Bethlehem of Judea, shepherds in the East witnessed an amazing phenomenon in the sky. These sheepherders had spent enough time stargazing while guarding their sheep to agree that tonight was different. In fact, it was magical when the Morning Star appeared in the sky. Then an angel appeared to them:

> And lo the angel of the Lord came upon them, and the glory of the Lord shone round about them: and they were afraid (Luke 2:9).

> And the angel said unto them, "Fear not: for behold, I bring you good tidings of great joy, which shall be to all people (Luke 2:10).

> "For unto you is born this day in the city of David a Savior, which is Christ the Lord (Luke 2:11).

> "And this shall be a sign unto you: Ye shall find the babe wrapped in swaddling clothes; lying in a manger" (Luke 2:12).

And suddenly there was with the angel a multitude of the heavenly host praising God and saying, (Luke 2:13)

"Glory to God in the highest, and on earth peace, goodwill toward men!" (Luke 2:14).

The shepherds quickly gathered their belongings, left their sheep in the safekeeping of their friends, and took off for Bethlehem. They were guided by the star they saw in the night sky, the same star they saw while they encircled their sheep and kept each other awake with stories. Now that star led them directly to Bethlehem, to the place where Mary and Jesus were staying. The shepherds were excited and spread the news along the way to every ear that would hear and every town that would listen. What a way to witness to others that the Savior was born, and they were on their way to see Him.

This is a great place to pause and focus on the word **Savior**. What does the word Savior really mean to you?

Word search: **Savior** (*Strong's Concordance* # 4990). This word means rescuer, redeemer, and liberator. The ancient Greeks used this word to refer to their gods and to humans who did good deeds.

It is okay to take a detour and check out sources within the other books of the Bible that chronicle how YHWH, God, our Lord and Savior is of a different caliber from other, minor gods. The promised Messiah would rescue fallen humanity by selecting a special group of people to whom he would demonstrate his attributes. He would have them sit for about four hundred years while he waited for another group of people to realize that they were not forgotten. He had indeed opened the door for the rest of the world to come in. He is the ultimate Lord and liberator. His message of liberation is the backbone of the Old Testament: Savior.

Jesus is the savior to bring Israel and Judah's old enemies—Assyria, Babylon, Moab, Edom, and Amon— to their knees. He is the savior who made a path through the Red Sea and gathered his people at the foot of Mt. Sinai. That journey was one of transformation for many who crossed the Red Sea and for their leader, Moses, and his team as well. Many, including Moses, never made it all the way to the land of promise, a reality check for all of us. It is because of God's mercies that we are not all consumed. The Lord renews His mercies every morning, all because of His faithfulness to the sons of men (Lamentations 3:22–23). He would always leave a remnant to tell the story of His saving grace and tender mercies.

I know the stories of ancient times can be rough, but they are still relevant. If you can handle it, take another detour with me. When you read about a man cutting up his dead wife's body into twelve parts and sending a part to each of the twelve tribes of Israel to emphasize the perversion among the tribe of Benjamin, it makes you cringe, doesn't it? Now, turn the pages to the book of Isaiah, read chapters 11 and 12 aloud, and say: This is what Luke 3:22 is talking about. "And the Holy Ghost descended in bodily form, like a dove upon Him, and a voice came from heaven which said, 'Thou art my beloved Son; in thee I am well pleased' (Matthew 3:17; Matthew 17:5).

He demonstrates the correct response to sin and all its temptations through self-control. Christ could only have done this through the empowerment of the Holy Spirit, the third person of the Godhead. This is the "stuff" of life. It is all good. I take some liberty with a huge smile when I say this to you only: This is "stinking sweet" because the Old Testament can be rough.

The scribes were blatant in recording the calamities that took place in ancient times and in detailing how God delivered them, such that many New Testament churches wanted no part of it. I say, take the whole or have no part of it. In any Bible study, take the time to apply what I call the *Berean approach*: Spend time searching the Scriptures. Treat it like you are going on going on an exploration. Just don't go deep sea diving in the books that were closed. They are historical but not inspirational.

The tradition of circumcision

ONE COMPLICATION FOR newborns is bleeding. Vitamin K helps prevent bleeding but does not cross the placenta during pregnancy. Studies have shown that giving Vitamin K to newborns within the first six hours after birth helps to speed up the process of blood coagulation.

In the Jewish tradition, the practice of circumcision or the Brit Mila ceremony, is done around the eighth day after a baby's birth in keeping with the law of Moses.

"And when eight days were accomplished for the circumcising of the child, his name was called Jesus, which was so named of the Angel before he was conceived in the womb" (Luke 2:21).

Like Elisabeth and Zacharias, Mary and Joseph insisted their baby should be called by the name the angel Gabriel assigned to them. Steeped in tradition, neither of these couples allowed anyone else to inform their decision.

Newborn circumcision shifted from homes to hospital wards largely due to infections such as the Manhattan Eastside outbreak reported to the New York City Sanitary Inspector by Dr. Abraham Jacobi in 1873. With reformation of some Jewish traditions and modernity, circumcision is now a choice. The New York Court of Appeals allowed hospitals to permit Jewish mohels, pious Jews well educated in performing the ritual in accordance with their faith, to perform circumcision under more sanitized conditions.

It is stimulating for me to compare some of these ancient ritual surrounding women, infants, and children because my twenty-year tenure working in obstetrics and gynecology was so rewarding. Back then it was unheard of for women to leave the hospital within twenty-four hours of delivery. Their stay was a minimum of two weeks because the recovery period for both mothers and babies was critical to their survival. Family-centered care was a later derivative of those observations.

Circumcision aside, what of the names the Angel Gabriel instructed these boys were to be called? Would their parents change them and use traditional names?

Postpartum purification

BLOOD IS THE SYMBOL of life and of purification. The seventh day also marks the end of the menstrual cycle and bleeding after having a baby. If the baby is a boy, the mother is considered impure for seven days; if she delivers a girl, the time is doubled to fourteen days. Scholars have attempted to theorize the reasons for this variance in length of impurity. However, nothing of what I have read makes sense to someone who has worked in obstetrics for twenty years. Perhaps men just needed more time to grieve the fact that the baby was a girl and not a boy. The male ego is at work within cultures when men lay the blame for a female birth on the woman. What is sad about such baloney is that only males possess an X and a Y chromosome. Women only possesses a double X (XX) chromosome. You don't need further calculations to determine which gender carries the deciding chromosome!

The lengths of time and the treatment for impurities were given to Moses by our Sovereign Lord. Every law and ordinance the lawgiver gave was relative to the covenant He made with Moses, the Mosaic Covenant. God knows all about us: Genesis 16:13 and Proverbs 15:38. Mary and Joseph were well instructed in these laws, and as such, they remained faithful in their religious practices.

Mary returned home and continued to do what all new mothers do: nurture and care for the newborn baby. I enjoyed watching my son-in-law as the good dad he is. He woke up when it was time for his wife to breastfeed their baby. First, he helped her settle in a rocking chair; then he would bring her a glass of water to drink. It did not matter that he had to go to work the next morning. He is a devoted husband and a doting dad.

Under the Mosaic regulations, my daughter would have been sent to the Red Tent, in the care of older women and away from her husband. There, she would have remained ceremonially unclean for the next thirty-three days, if the baby was a female. Since her baby was a male, her isolation period had to be seven days longer.

Outside of this tradition, women in our culture are not having it. I had to use lots of wisdom when I worked labor and delivery. Often a nurse can discern whether the supporting partner is likely to become another patient or if the person is becoming weak and sweaty. This is a perfect time to suggest getting a snack, a drink of water, taking a break, and to switch positions from the foot of the bed to its head. There he can support her through breathing and relaxation rather than faint at the sight of the miracle of childbirth. Some handle it well, but some just can't, and the nurse needs to determine that early in the game unless she wants to take care of two patients. (That was a bit tangential but relevant.) The old and the new ways of doing things often remain controversial for generations.

The covenant also demanded that the couple present their firstborn infant to God, for every firstborn belongs to Him (Exodus 13:2, 12; Numbers 18:6; 1 Samuel 1:2). This occurred forty days post-delivery and was significant for Mary because she could sacrifice for her Lord. At that time, she could offer a sacrifice of a lamb or two birds, if she could not afford to buy a lamb:

> And the Lord spoke to Moses, saying,
>
> Speak to the children of Israel, saying: If a woman has conceived and born a man child: then she shall be unclean seven days; as in the days; according to the days of the separation for her infirmity shall she be unclean.
>
> And on the eighth day, the flesh of his foreskin shall be circumcised.
>
> She shall then continue in the blood of her purification for thirty-three days. She shall not touch any hallowed thing nor come into the sanctuary until the days of her purification are fulfilled.
>
> (Leviticus 12:1–4)

Luke adamantly reminds us that the main characters are faithful people. They held their premise, and God would keep His promise to each of them. Joseph and Mary are like any other family today; they had just paid the property tax, spent money on travel, and had unexpected expenses staying over as guests with family. Joseph was from Bethlehem. They were likely a middle-class family, low on cash, and didn't have credit cards back then. Moreover, borrowing money to purchase the lamb required for this sacred occasion would have impacted Joseph's self-esteem. Perhaps he would feel such a sacrifice would not be authentic.

Mary was very young, but she was wise. She was not quite yet the helpmate for her husband described in Proverbs 31. She respected his decision to stay within the budget and to buy what he could afford: two pigeons. They would offer their sacrifice according to the law of the Lord and traditions passed down to them: a pair of turtle doves or two young pigeons (Leviticus 12: 8; Luke 2:24).

Mary was happy to be back in the temple. This was their first time back in temple worship. This tradition is still taken seriously in many parts of the world. Many churches remain divided on the dogma of infant baptism. Mary and Joseph did not have these Tertulian issues but they had problems of their own.

Chapter 7

Simeon and Anna

"But they that wait upon the Lord shall renew their strength; they shall mount up with wings as eagles; they shall run, and not be wear; and they shall walk, and not faint" (Isaiah 40:31).

Mary was on her way to the Temple nursery when she heard the heard shuffling steps behind her. She stopped dead in her tracks. She recognized old Simeon. While he was formally introducing himself to Mary, the Holy Ghost came upon him. He took the child Jesus up in his arms and blessed him, saying,

> Lord, now lettest thou thy servant depart in peace, according to thy word: For mine eyes have seen thy salvation, Which thou hast prepared before the face of all people; A light to lighten the Gentiles and the glory of thy people Israel (Luke 2:26–32).

Simeon was not rude, but in his response to the sight of Mary and Joseph entering the temple, he felt a resurgence of youthful energy. He bustled through the crowd and gave an oral rendition of the prophet Isaiah, fulfilling God's promise to him through the Holy Spirit: "That he would not see death before he has seen the Lord's Christ" (Luke 2:26).

Simeon carefully took the baby Jesus from his mother's arms and held him close, reciting the words of the prophet Isaiah: "The Lord hath made his holy arm in the eyes of all the nations, and all the ends of the earth shall see the salvation of our God" (Isaiah 52:10). After he blessed Christ Child, Simeon made his personal request to God: Nunc dimittis (Permit me to depart from this life). This was the song of Simeon's heart as he left the temple.

We can all learn a lesson from Simeon on how to wait on the promises of God. Before Simeon returned the Christ Child to his parents' arms, he blessed them and prophesied to Mary, saying,

> Behold, this child is set for the fall and rising again of many in Israel; and for a sign which will be spoken against.

> (Yea, a sword will pierce through thy own soul also), that the thoughts of many hearts may be revealed (Luke 2: 34–35).

Who was Anna?

ANNA. TOO, WAS IN THE temple, waiting for the fulfillment of the prophecy about the one who would come that she had read in the volumes of ancient Hebrew history. She had been waiting all her monastic life. Luke dedicates two whole verses to her credit. I am interested in her backstory.

Anna was another female figure to whom God would give credit for her life of dedication to him. She lived a righteous life. She followed the tradition of early marriage and was a widow at an early age, but she never remarried. This widow is another character who remained faithful to her Jewish customs. Luke traces her descendants back to the tribe of Asher.

Imagine the patriarch Israel (Jacob), on his deathbed surrounded by his twelve sons. "Gather together, that I may tell you what shall befall you in the last days" (Genesis 49:1–28). When Israel got to his eight sons who were born to Leah's handmaid, Zilpah, he said, "Bread from Ashur (Assur) shall be rich. And he shall yield royal dainties" (Genesis 49:20). It came to pass that Asher was one of the most prosperous of the twelve tribes of Israel. Ashur remained unified with his brothers after entering the Promised Land until Solomon's death around the middle of the tenth century BC when the United Monarchy was divided into two kingdoms. Ashur and his tribe joined the nine others who took control of the Northern Kingdom, making Samaria their capital. The two remaining tribes, Judah and Benjamin, took hold of the City of Jerusalem, the home of Solomon's temple, and the southern territories of Ephraim (Genesis 35:37).

For more than 200 years, the tribe of Ashur remained a part of the Northern Kingdom until they were conquered by the Assyrians in 722 BC during the reign of King Hoshea (from 732–722 BC). The Assyrian conquest began the subsequent dispersion of the ten northern tribes. Today, historians classify the northern tribes as the ten lost tribes of Israel. Many fled to the Southern Kingdom until Judah was defeated by the Babylonians in 532 BC, leaving all twelve tribes displaced.

But Luke dug deep into history and identified Anna as a direct descendant of the tribe of Asher. That is deep dedication to the cause of Jesus Christ! This Gentile was serious about telling the world that the Savior has come, and His name is JESUS CHRIST.

Anna is one of nine prophetesses mentioned in the Bible. Ancient writing designated women as prophetesses if their husbands were prophets; examples are Hulda, the wife of Shallum (2 Chronicles 34:22), and the wife of the prophet Isaiah (Isaiah 8:3). The two other prophetesses given a notable mention in the Old Testament are Miriam, the sister of Moses and Aaron (Exodus 15:20) and Judge Deborah (Judges 4:4).

> And there was one, Anna, a prophetess, the daughter of Phanuel, of the tribe of (Aser) Asher: She was of a great age and had lived with a husband seven years from her virginity. And she was a widow of about eighty-four years; who did not depart from the temple but served God with fasting and prayers night and day. And coming in that instant she gave thanks to the Lord; and spoke of Him to all those who looked for redemption in Jerusalem (Luke 2:36–38).

The New Testament mentions mention the four unnamed daughters of Philip as prophetesses in (Acts 21:19).

Luke tells us that Anna became a widow after only seven years of marriage. Young Anna never remarried; instead, she lived a liturgical life. She was quite content to in her humble quarters for young widows, and was completely dedicated to temple services Perhaps Her life was like that of a modern-day nun living in a convent where she listens for the tolling bell, signifying it is time to drop her monastic chores and head to the temple for set liturgical prayers: sunrise prayers (Prime), noon day (Sext), afternoon (None), at sunset (Vespers), and bedtime (Compline).

Anna was spending more time praying and fasting than dining out with her young friends. She would become well known around campus for foretelling of the promised Kingdom Redeemer who would come and save Israel. She was a source of solace to her community. There is a difference between forth telling and foretelling, so jot down these words and look them up at leisure.

Anna was eighty-four years old when Mary and Joseph brought Jesus to the temple for his dedication (Numbers 6:2). Bible scholars still debate her actual age; for if she had been widowed for eighty-four years when Jesus appeared for his bar mitzvah at thirteen, she would have been ninety-seven years old. Seriously!

There is no record in the Bible of Anna's date of birth or the date of her wedding; given those two unknowns, Anna would have been somewhere between ninety-seven and one hundred and three years old. These calculations are based on ancient

Roman scholars who postulated that the median age for girls to be given for marriage was as young as twelve.

Here we see Anna as a recipient of God's favor, at one hundred and three hurrying to the temple as Mary and Joseph enter. She shouts with glee as Mary and Joseph enter the temple. Anna begins to give thanks for the fulfillment of her prophetic words as the Holy Ghost gives her utterance to all those present and who are waiting for the Christ Child.

John introduces Jesus

THIS IS THE KINSMAN Redeemer, who John introduced as the spotless Lamb of God as he saw Jesus walking toward him. "Behold the lamb of God which taketh away the sin of the world" (John 1:29).

The song "Behold, the Lamb of God" comes to mind immediately. I felt the presence of the Holy Spirit, a gentle reminder that there was passion in their patience. They never gave in, neither did they give up; they just knew the day would come. At last! It did.

Years ago, Juanita Bynum penned a song titled "I Don't Mind Waiting." I was passionately waiting for miraculous healing for my six-year-old grandbaby. I still don't mind waiting on the Lord. If it is not His will, I still trust Him. I encourage everyone who is sick in body, mind, or soul, to make all the changes you can in nutrition and lifestyle; live a clean and righteous life like Anna and Simeon, and trust God to do the rest.

Mary would experience heartache as her baby's role in God's redemption plan played out before her eyes. She would witness the pain of His crucifixion and rejection by his own people. "He came unto his own, and his own received him not ..." (John1:11–13).

There is a gap or space in the development of the Jesus story from the time his parents presented him for purification until the time of return. I am impelled by the Holy Spirit and my own volition to use this gap to explore Anna's descendants back to Noah and the reason for the hope she cherished.

Backstory: Noah and his family were the only human survivors of the flood that destroyed the earth. According to first-century historian Flavius Josephus, Shem, Noah's third son, had five sons whose children occupied all the territories along the Euphrates River extending as far as the Indian Ocean. The descendants of Shem's five sons were:

Elam – Elamites who occupied Persia

Ashur (Asser) – Assyrians who occupied Nieve and who were Anna ancestors

Arphaxad – The Arphaxadites now known as the Chaldeans

Aram – The Aramites, whom the Greeks called Syrians

Heber – Progenitor of the Hebrew people; occupied much of Asia

Heber fathered Joctan and Phaleg. Joctan had thirteen boys, and their descendants also occupied territories along the Indian River. It was Phaleg's son Ragau, who fathered Serug who fathered Nahor, who fathered Terah who was the father of Abraham.

Now Abraham had two half-brothers, Nahor and Haran. Haran died, leaving two daughters and one son. Nahor married his niece, Milcah, and Abe married his niece, Sarai. According to Josephus (Antiquities 1.6.), Terah detested the national attention Haran received at his death, so they decided to relocate.

Abram's stargazing obsession with mysticism would lead him on a quest. He wanted to know which one of the gods the Chaldean people held in high esteem. But he wanted to know for himself the God who was behind all of this magnificence. Abram—God would change his name to Abraham—reminds me of John called Baptist, who would also be the forerunner or messenger of the Greater One to come. Abe would evangelize on the premise of the existence of just one God who was greater than his hirelings. John the Baptist ran on the premise he was not worthy to unlatch the sandals on the feet of the man coming after him (Luke 3:16).

The Chaldeans, however, grew wary of Abram's obsession with theocracy and with his father's disdain for the culture as well. Terah, Abe's dad, took his entire family, including the newlyweds, and moved to Haran of Mesopotamia. This is important because Terah would die there, and God would call Abram to serve him there. He would instruct him to go to

Canaan and seal his transition with a name change (Genesis 17:5). Abraham would become a wealthy man and would need an heir to whom he could pass down his legacy. His nephew, Lot, was like a son; his servant was closer to him than his nephew, but Abe wanted a kid. The problem was age and infertility: but Abe and Sarai were getting old. God would send an angel to visit Abram, just as the Angel Gabriel later visited Zacharias, and announced that he would be the father of many nations and that he would father a son.

> And the Lord appeared unto him in the plains of Mamre: and he sat in the tent door in the heat of the day.

> And he lifted up his eyes and looked, and lo, three men stood by him: and when he saw them, he ran to meet them from the tent door and bowed himself toward the ground.

> And said, My Lord, if now I have found favor in thy sight, pass not away, I pray thee, from thy servant (Genesis 18:1–3).

The divine manifestation of the deity of God to man is a tangible form called a theophany. The word originates in Latin, *theophania*, and links two concepts: *Theos*, meaning God, and *phainein*, "bring to light, to shine or cause light to appear."

Why is this extensive backstory important? God made a covenant with Abraham and his progenitors based on obedience and forgiveness through animal sacrifice. Each generation would break the covenant and worship other gods (idolatry). Their behaviors had become so offensive to God that He repented and made man multiple times. God made an oath (rainbow and the seasons) that he would never destroy the earth by flood again, He used other nations to judge His people. God would give them peace under leaders that He would raise up and appoint to be His voice to the nation of Israel.

The nation would rest from wars under King David and his predecessor, King Solomon, his son by marriage to Uriah's widow, Bathsheba. Unlike his father, Solomon was an idol worshipper whose lust for idolatrous women infuriated God. God told him, in today's vernacular, *I would have ripped the kingdom from your hands a long time ago had it not been for your father, David.* The Lord would spare the king but not his sons. The kingdom was divided after Solomon's death during the rule of his sons; Jeroboam ruled in the North (Israel) and Rehoboam in the South over Judah. The first discipline came in 538 BC when the Southern Kingdom fell to the Assyrians.

The Northern Kingdom, Israel, fell to the Babylonians in 722 BC. King Nebuchadnezzar took them to Babylon as captives and held them for seventy years. Some remained faithful to God, and others assimilated by marrying foreign wives and worshipping the gods of their captors.

Those who remained faithful would pass on the religious life, customs, and traditions to their offspring. All they had to live by was their hope in God, YHWH. The one true God the prophets foretold would come and redeem them once and for all. This was the premise Simeon, Anna, Zacharias and Elisabeth, and young Joseph and Mary stood on all their lives.

This song, "One Day," written by J. Wilbur Chapman (1859–1918), embraces the theology of the redemptive work Jesus Christ would accomplish.

One day when heaven was filled with His praises,

One day, when sin was as black as could be,

Jesus came forth to be born of a virgin,

Dwelt among men, my example is He!

Refrain:

Living, he loved me, dying he saved me:

Buried, he carried my sins far away;

Rising, he justified freely, forever;

One day he's coming:

O Glorious day!

One day they left Him alone in the garden,

One day he rested from suffering free;

Angels came down o'er His tomb to keep vigil;

Hope of the hopeless, my savior

Refrain

One day, the grave could conceal him no longer,

One day, the stones rolled away from the door,

Then He arose, over death,

He had conquered,

Now is ascended, my Lord, evermore!

Refrain

One day, the trumpet will sound for His coming,

One day, the skies with His glory will shine:

Wonderful day, my beloved ones bringing;

Glorious Savior, this Jesus is mine!

Refrain

(African Methodist Episcopal Church Hymnal, # 490.

Jesus would wrap Himself in light and enter the matrix of humanity, imputing the sin of mankind upon Himself. What a mighty God we serve!

In our discourse, we have captured the reason for Simeon and Anna's hope in fulfilling a kinsman Redeemer through the birth of John the Baptist. John was the forerunner or messenger who did the foretelling of the one who would come after him. The boys—John and Jesus—grew up playing cops and robbers for the first two years of their lives. Eventually, they caught the attention of King Herod. The word on the street was that wise men were at the gate, inquiring about a lad born a couple of years ago. They may have said: *We are so sorry we could not have gotten here sooner but, your royal highness, we are coming all the way from Egypt.*

The king appeared unconvinced at the moment that a mere child could present a threat to his throne. *Guards, take their camels and give them a room in the palace for the night. They will be on their way in the morning.* And so, it was.

But Herod had a troubling history. He would hear voices in his head every time he saw a young boy: *This is the one who is going to get your th-ro-ne,* in a mocking drawl. His close confidantes noticed the king had trouble sleeping and would become verbally obsessed with jealousy about this unknown kid to the point of becoming delusional. No amount of bloodletting or purging would cure his melancholy. Finally, unable to cope with the thought of losing his position, he issued an edict to kill all infants two years and under. This narrative is recorded in Matthew's telling written to a Jewish audience unlike Luke's, which was written to a Gentile audience. I believe both authors did a brilliant job of presenting two different perspectives to the story about the birth of Jesus and life.

Dr. Luke picks up after Jesus's purification where Simeon and Anna doted on the baby who would one day become the King of Kings. Joseph, Mary, and baby Jesus returned through rough terrain, steep hillside, and lush mountains back to southern Judah in the lower regions of Galilee to a town called Nazareth. Luke noted, "And the Child grew and became strong in spirit, filled with wisdom, and the grace of God was upon Him" (Luke 2:40).

Every year Joseph would make the long journey of 148 kilometers from Nazareth to Jerusalem for the Passover Feast. This is where Luke picks up with the return of a twelve-year-old Jesus, although Joseph may have gone up with other men for Passover Feast (Exodus 23:14–17; Luke 2:41–51).

Jesus transitions into adulthood

NOW TWELVE-YEAR-OLD Jesus is ready to participate in a deeper understanding of his Jewish tradition. After the Feast, Mary and Joseph linked up with friends and family to begin the pilgrimage back to Nazareth. After the first day of the journey, Joseph went among the cousins to hang out with the boys and to check on his boys discretely, but Jesus was not among them.

"Now it was after three days they found him in the temple, sitting in the midst of teachers—Jewish rabbis. Jesus was both listening to them and asking questions" (Luke 4:46). Jesus was central and was engaged in a philosophical conversation as if he were one of them.

His parents were impressed by his abilities. *This is unreal*, Mary may have whispered to his father. Then she remembered the agony he had caused them, and her angry mama side kicked in. *Little Boy, come here.* She might have pointed her index finger at him, curling it back and forth into the shape of the letter C while giving him that stern look that said *Son, you know you don't want me to come and get you!* Jesus got the message and went to his mother. Finally, she may have said, *"Do you have any idea how worried your father and I have been? And here you are, continuing with your conversation after you saw us, as if we are not your parents? Son, why have you done this to us? Your father and I have sought You anxiously"* (Luke 2:48).

Without flinching, Mary's little boy looked her dead in the eye and spoke like a man: "Why did you seek me?" (Luke 2:49).

Huh ,she may have said, likely clenching her fist beneath her shawl in righteous indignation. Jesus continued to sass her with his retort, "Did you not know that I must be about My Father's business?" (Luke 2:49).

This lad needed an eye exam. *Jesus, your father is right here! We were both looking for you!* For a split second, she had a knee-jerking recollection of her angelic encounter with Gabriel. Mary made an attitude adjustment. She mentally flipped the lid of the upper chambers of her heart where she had tucked the message she had received from Angel Gabriel; there she added this scenario. Of all the children she would give birth to, this boy, Jesus, would be very different.

On the way home, his father kept him by his side. He talked to him like any loving father would. *Son, I love you very much. I don't know what your life will be, but I know YWHW has a plan for your life* (Jeremiah 29:11). *But as long as you are under my roof, you are subjected to my rules as your earthly father; so, don't ever get that twisted again.*

Jesus would remain obedient to his earthly parents, whom God placed as guardians. He watched his father work hard and build his own carpentry business. He wrestled and played with his siblings, his cousins, and his childhood friends, who were all a part of a stable Jewish community of believers. "And Jesus increased in wisdom, stature, and favor with God and men" (Luke 2:52).

I implore you to continue this study on the life and ministry of Jesus Christ as narrated in the book of Luke. Have these discussion with others, ask hard questions, feel free to diverge in wonderment or conversation—but always come back and dissect it with Scriptures. You will find thoughts, ideas, and passages you may not agree with or are not interpreted according to your theology. I encourage you to send me a kind email and I can share my thoughts. I am here to declare that I am not a debater or an apologist by trade, but I can depend on the Holy Spirit to enlighten me with a Godly response from His Word.

For those who believe the Christmas story is a hoax and December twenty-fifth is just another pagan-oriented reason to celebrate, go back and research the months of the year according to the Hebrew and Gregorian calendars. The sixth month in the Hebrew calendar, Elul, is the third month in the Gregorian calendar introduced by Pope Gregory XIII (1582). Elul would be the twelfth month in the Jewish calendar (Rosh Hashana). This places the birth of Christ nine months later, around the month of December.

If all else fails, pick any of the twelve months of the year and celebrate Jesus Christ because he was born. The early church had problems with the excessive "leap days," as they were called, because they threw off the astronomical calculations of the time for Passover. These discrepancies with the Julian calendar were discussed and settled at the first Nicaean Council in AD 325. The original creed has been changed in a few areas over the years to reflect the "Christian" church in place of the "Catholic" church. I wanted to add a copy of the original Creed here and also the addition to the Creed. The sale of it on the internet reflects the sale of indulgencies in the time of Erasmus and Martin Luther. I opted out of such indulgences. Growing up in the British Commonwealth with religion as a vital part of our education, learning to recite the Nicaean creed was a given. I am grateful for that foundation.

A Benediction

Now may joy of the Christmas story bring, to you and your household, the joy of a daily practice to live the victorious life Christ offered to humanity. Now Go! Find somebody and tell them about Jesus.

Sources

BBC History. *Augustus (63 BC–AD 14)*. https://www.bbc.co.uk/history/historic_figures/ augustus.shtml. Retrieved 01/20/2024.

Boogert, Ernst (2015?). *The Origin of the Byzantine Text: New Perspectives in a Deadlock Debate.* https://www.academia.edu/10303182/ The_Origin_of_the_Byzantine_Text_New_Perspectives_in_a_D

Breshears. Jefrey D. (2017). *Introduction to Bibliology: What Every Christian Should Know about the Origins, Composition, Inspiration, Interpretation, Canonicity, and Transmission of the Bible.* Wipf and Stock.

Chester, Craig (2016). Monterey Institute for Research and Astronomy. https://www.mira.org. Retrieved 02/24/2025.

Cunningham, Lawrence and Ignatius Charles Brady. "St. Francis of Assisi," Britannica. https://www.britannica.com/biography/ Saint-Francis-of-Assisi. Retrieved 01/11/2024.

Josephus, Flavius. *The Antiquities of the Jews,"* translated by William Whiston.

https://www.gutenberg.org/files/2848/2848-h/
2848-h.htm.

J. Wilbur Chapman. "One Day," *African Methodist
Episcopal Church Hymnal # 490.*

Rydelnik, Michael. "Why is Joseph important to
Jesus genealogy?" Today in the Word.
https://www.todayintheword.org/question-and-
answer/why-is-joseph-important-to-jesus-
genealogy/ Retrieved 01/18/2024.

Tanakh (Ketuvin, the Jewish Bible) (1985). Jewish
Publication Society.

White, James R. (2009). *The King James Only
Controversy: Can You Trust Modern Translations?*
Bethany House.

My Inspiration for This book

About the Author

DR. GRACE DAVIDSON is a Christian and aspiring author, speaker, and teacher. She holds the Doctor in Ministry degree from Beacon University, a Master of Education degree and a Master of Science in Counseling and Psychology degree from Troy University, and a Bachelor of Science degree from Augusta State University.

She has been a Registered Professional Nurse for over forty years and is a proud Diploma graduate of University Hospital of the West Indies School of Nursing. Her vocation has been one huge and wonderful ministry and, outside of grandparenting, the most rewarding.

Dr. Grace continues to serve through her local church. She also serves national and international communities through Christian organizations.

Like these characters in Luke's narrative, God will use your and your most unusual circumstances to accomplish His will, if you just trust Him.